EMOTIONAL
FIRST AID

A Field Guide to
Crisis Intervention
and
Psychological Survival

COL James L. Greenstone
EdD, JD, DABECI

wholeperson
Stress & Wellness Publishers
Duluth, Minnesota

Whole Person
101 W. 2nd St., Suite 203
Duluth, MN 55802

800-247-6789

books@wholeperson.com
www.wholeperson.com

**Emotional First Aid: A Field Guide
to Crisis Intervention and Psychological Survival**

You may photocopy the contents of Appendix A.
A CD is available from Whole Person Associates containing
a PDF file that includes all of Appendix A for easy printing.
This may not be purchased unless you have or will have
purchased the book. Call Whole Person Associates at
800-247-6789 to order your CD or find it on our website
at the bottom of the Emotional First Aid page.

Printed in the United States of America

Editor: Peg Johnson
Art Director: Joy Morgan Dey

Library of Congress Cataloging in Publication Data

2015938676

ISBN: 978-157025-329-4

Guiding Principle

The fate of the emotionally wounded
rests in the hands of the one who does
the initial Crisis Intervention.

The Field Guide to Emotional First Aid *is dedicated
to my partner of 35 years, Dr. Sharon Cohen Leviton,
to my mentor of 40 years, Dr. Edward Stephen Rosenbluh,
and to all those who came before and prepared the way
for this vital discipline that is part of our lives today.
Further, it is dedicated to those who will effectively administer
Crisis Intervention through utilization of what
follows in this Guide.*

Foreword

Emotional First Aid: A Field Guide to Crisis Intervention and Psychological Survival fully covers subject matter not addressed in full elsewhere. It is:

- Timely
- Clearly and concisely written
- User friendly
- Full of charts, graphs, lists, etc. to serve as quick references and supplements.

The most important feature of the book is the professional integrity and reliability of its author, Dr. James L. Greenstone. His strength and sure-footedness are in evidence throughout.

It has been my privilege to work with Dr. Greenstone for thirty-five years. In 1978, I attended a five-day conference sponsored by the National Institute for Training in Crisis Intervention held in Louisville, Kentucky. Students of Crisis Management, regardless of professional credentials, could receive specific, expert training. Dr. Greenstone and Dr. Edward S. Rosenbluh were the Institute co-directors and lead instructors. The quality of the training was impressive. Following the conference Dr. Greenstone and I created a partnership that has continued to focus on studying, teaching, training, and publishing in crisis management, mediation, negotiation and other areas of dispute resolution. Please refer to the author's biography at the end of the book for a more complete listing of Dr. Greenstone's professional affiliations.

My respect for Dr. Greenstone's integrity is based on observations that span many years. He immerses himself in whatever he undertakes and remains on task and on schedule. He possesses an insatiable intellectual curiosity. His interests, studies and professional involvements cut across multiple disciplines. He has an expansive world view, but can move with ease to focus in on the particular. He is able to compartmentalize and to reduce verbal clutter and extraneous talk. This is particularly helpful in the assessment phase of a crisis situation where being able to identify the core crisis is crucial. Dr. Greenstone calls upon his studies, his research, his extensive experience, and his creativity to find innovative ways to teach, to challenge, to remain current, and to think ahead. He has honed this book to a fine point, keeping what is needed and avoiding what is not. The issue of cause and effect is paramount in his teaching. As he tells responders, "Always have a reason for what you do. Reacting rather than responding can serve to heighten the stress and sabotage the intervention."

Take a moment to write the following words on a card and attach the card to your responder notebook. The words are: PREPARE…PREPARE…PREPARE.

Being a responder regardless of your particular agency affiliation carries with it a sacred trust. That trust begins with an expectation that the responder will demonstrate an appropriate level of preparation, competency, training and mental and physical fitness for the task. Waiting until the last minute is not preparation. Dr. Greenstone includes a comprehensive section on the need for ongoing preparation. You cannot be a trusted professional responder without incorporating this information in your approach.

Emotional First Aid is carefully crafted to assist the reader. It is a major resource at a time when the need for trained responders is urgent. Your service is honorable. You deserve the gratitude of those who depend on you.

— Sharon C. Leviton, PhD

Author's Note

This is a *Field Guide* for behavioral health first and second responders. Novices to those with years of experience will find information to help them answer the call to emergencies more effectively. More and more behavioral healthcare professionals and paraprofessionals are being asked to leave the relative comfort of their regular workplace and to work in disaster scenarios. Just because you may be ready and willing to go does not mean, in and of itself, that you are prepared to go. Here you will find many of those preparation and response concerns addressed. Direction is given and many forms and guidelines are provided to help make your experience in this relatively new venue a rewarding one. Being unprepared will distract from your mission, your satisfaction, and steer you away from making such responses in the future.

This book addresses:

1. Basic Crisis Intervention / emotional first aid procedures.

2. Force protection procedures and resiliency information.

3. Information for adjusting one's mindset to the disaster scenario.

4. What to take with you when you go.

5. Special concerns about which each responder should be aware.

6. Reproducible reference forms, tests and tables for use before, during and after responding to critical situations.

Acknowledgments

Sharon Cohen Leviton, PhD, DABECI – My Partner and Chief Critic

Edward Steven Rosenbluh, PhD, DABECI – My Mentor

Suzanne Nardecchia Raif, BA – My Right Arm

W. Rodney Fowler, EdD, PhD, DABECI – My Teacher

The Texas State Guard Medical Brigade – My Military Team

BG Luis Fernandez, MD – My Commanding Officer

Texas 4, Disaster Medical Assistance Team – My Federal Team

Karen Ray, PhD – My Student

Col Charles R. Bauer, MD – My Supporter

CSM William Campbell – My Command Sergeant Major

Pamela Celeste Greenstone, MA, LPC – My daughter who inspired parts
   of this book.

CPT Nancy Nagel – My Friend

COL Robert Morecook, PhD – My Advisor

LTC James Ray Hays, PhD – My Colleague

MG Marshall Scantlin – My Guide

The Honorable Dub Bransom – My Constable

Chief Deputy Constable Fred Rogers – My Chief

Weldon Walles – My Back

Marissa Y. Martinez-Collins – My Spanish Language Consultant

María Isabel López – My Spanish Language Consultant

Contents

Chapter 1

Traumatic Crisis and Its Aftermath: What are we up against?

Remember and never forget:
Understanding the situation is vital to response.

Crisis is in the eye of the beholder. Crisis involves stress; unusual stress that renders the sufferer unable to cope with their life as they usually would. A disaster exists when the resources available to address the emergency are less than those required to address the needs of the victims and the overall situation. A disaster can be of any size. Overwhelmed resources equals a disaster as differentiated from an emergency in which adequate resources can be utilized to resolve or to manage the needs of those affected. This guide will discuss crisis and the effect of overwhelmed resources both personal and public.

The crisis trilogy presents a way of understanding the causation in crisis situations. The trilogy involves events occurring that are:

1. Sudden in onset

2. Unexpected by the victim or their significant others

3. Apparently arbitrary in nature

All three are major sources of unusual stress. Because crisis is in the eye of the beholder, what is unusual stress for one may not be unusual for another. The Crisis Cube, on page 4, helps to understand this concept. The level of functioning overall, the presence or absence of functional emotional problems, and the experience handling stress and similar daily life behaviors can be a determiner of a person's susceptibility to experiencing

FIGURE 1.1.   PSYCHOLOGICAL STRUCTURING
External and internal factors in a social stimulus situation.
(Sherif and Sherif, 1956)

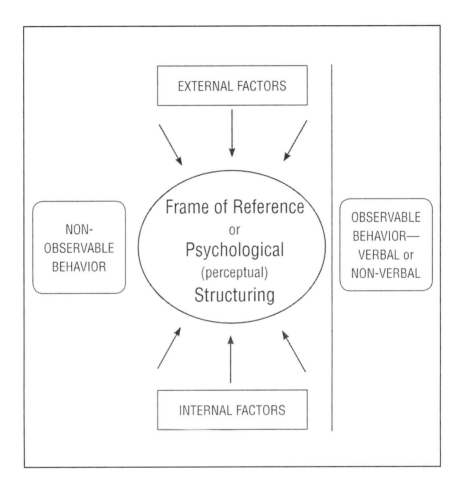

External Factors	Internal Factors
Objects	Motives
Cultural products	Attitudes
Person	Emotions
Groups	Various states of the organism
	Effects of past experiences

(Continued on the next page)

FIGURE 1.1. PSYCHOLOGICAL STRUCTURING (*Continued*)

Additionally, Sherif and Sherif (1948 and 1956) provided their basic and unyielding principles of social interaction that provide a background for our understanding of Crises and Emotional First Aid. The following are adaptations of these remarkable principles that Sherif believed apply in all social situations. The implications for understanding and for responding effectively to those in crisis can be easily seen. What we do is based on what we know about what the sufferer or victim is doing, thinking or experiencing.

1. Experience and behavior constitute a unity.

2. Behavior follows central psychological structuring. See Figure 1.1.

3. Psychological structuring is jointly determined by external and internal factors. See Figure 1.1.

4. Internal factors such as motives, attitudes, etc. and experience are inferred from behavior.

5. The psychological tendency is toward structuring of experience.

6. Structured stimulus situations set limits to alternatives in psychological structuring.

7. In unstructured stimulus situations, alternatives in psychological structuring are increased.

8. The more unstructured the stimulus situation, the greater the relative contribution of internal factors in the frame of reference.

9. The more unstructured the stimulus situation, the greater the relative contribution of external social factors in the frame of reference.

10. Various factors in the frame of reference have differing relative weights.

11. Psychological activity is selective.

12. Human psychological functioning is typically on the conceptual level. (Sherif and Sherif, 1948 and 1956).

crisis in their life at a particular time. No one is immune to crisis. Enough stress at the wrong time and in a particular person can mean crisis even for the strongest of us. This includes responders and crisis interveners as well. Sherif's (1956) principles described below are very helpful in understanding this and in preparing for such eventualities. See Figure 1.1 above.

FIGURE 1.2 – THE CRISIS CUBE

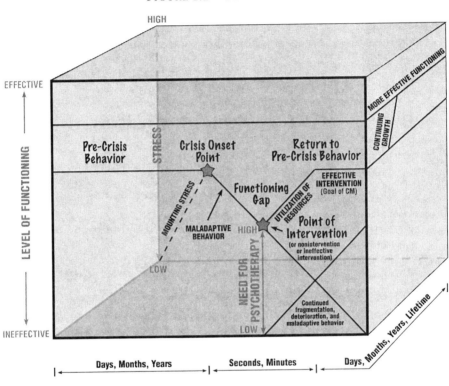

Within the crisis trilogy, suddenness refers to the way in which a person may encounter the stressful event or events leading to the possibility of crisis. For example, someone jumps out from behind a tree and attacks a passer-by. No delay, no warning, just the sudden attack. The passer-by may have walked this way many times without incident and has little expectation of problems. The problem occurs as described and was not expected; the second aspect of the trilogy. The third aspect of the trilogy asks, "Why me?" Of all the people to whom this could have happened, why did it happen to me? The concerns expressed can be a great source of added stress to the victim of an attack.

Taken together or even separately, these factors above can be a source of unusual stress capable of overwhelming the usual coping skills of the sufferer. When this trilogy is applied to the occurrence of a disaster, the crisis reactions become a little more predictable and understandable. And, in the same way, some victims will react and respond differently from others

FIGURE 1.3 – CRISIS VS CRISIS MANAGEMENT
How crises tend to emotionally shut down sufferers and how effective crisis management and emotional first aid can reverse the process.
(*Adapted form Evarts, Greenstone, et al, 1983*)

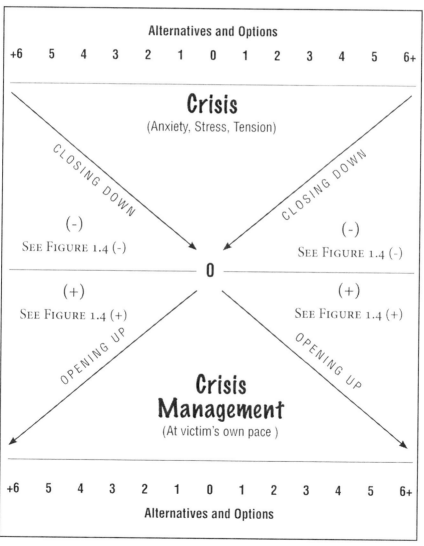

FIGURE 1.4. THE ELEMENTS OF CRISIS VS CRISIS MANAGEMENT

What happens during crisis (-)	What happens during crisis management or crisis intervention (+)
Tendency to close down emotionally.	Tendency to open up at sufferer's own pace.
Access to resources decreases.	Maladaptive behavior decreases.
Supports more difficult to access or unavailable.	Resource utilization increases.
Problem-solving ability decreases.	Problem solving skills increase.
Maladaptive behavior increases.	Access to or recognition of support systems increase.
Psychological growth is limited.	Possibilities for growth increase.
Possibility of physical violence escalates.	Chances of physical violence decrease.
Pre-crisis behavior inaccessible.	Likelihood of returning to pre-crisis behavior increases.
Difficulty seeing helpful possibilities.	Ability to get on with one's life increases.
Interactions close down.	Opens interactions with others.
Threats may increase.	Reduction in feelings of frustration.
Higher levels of frustration.	Decrease in threats.
Alternatives seem limited. (After the crisis)	Alternatives open up and can be recognized. (After the crisis)
Options seem limited. (During the crisis)	Options more readily available. (When dealing with the crisis)

based on the more or less personal resources available to them. For instance, someone who has gone through a crisis or a disaster previously, and has resolved or at least managed the issues that were involved in an effective manner, may be better able to cope in a new situation. Those who have used the "bandaid" approach to crisis management or to life's problems in general may have unresolved issues that will make the current experience more difficult to handle.

Those who effectively and successfully deal with high stress issues and personal problems when they occur, rather than denying or refusing to deal with them, often come through their present crisis in much better shape emotionally than those who do not. The need for additional and or ongoing counseling or psychotherapy after the fact may be minimized by this group as well. The effectiveness of the crisis intervention may be another important factor in this equation. The better we do now, the less we will probably have to do later.

Another crucial aspect of a crisis is that it will not go on forever. The human body and mind cannot handle crisis-level stress indefinitely. Crises

FIGURE 1.5 – THE CRISIS CONTINUUM
Increased direct contact with the disaster and the likelihood
of personal crisis.

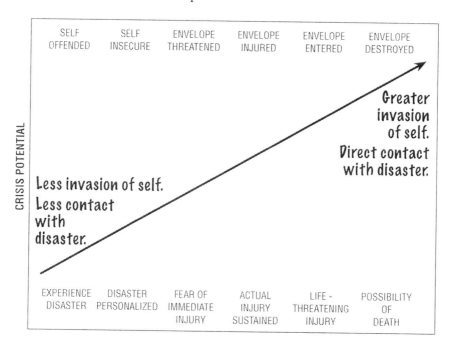

are self-limiting. If an intervener did nothing to assist the sufferer, the crisis would still end on its own. The issue then becomes the condition of the victim when the crisis has ended. The ultimate self-resolution, without intervention, could be death due to the body's need or the sufferer's need to end the pain caused by excessively heightened stress. Immediate and effective intervention that seeks to stop the downward spiral of maladaptive behavior will usually yield better results. An intervener who knows what to do as well as when and how much to do can prevent predictable outcomes to unresolved heightened stress and perhaps even reduce the need for professional psychological assistance later. **Figure 1.2, page 4,** helps to explain this relationship.

The pre-crisis functioning, either effective or not, of an individual has probably existed over a long period of time prior to the instant situation. The way previous crises have been handled, presence or absence of functional mental disorders, level of general daily function, adequacy of coping and survival skills, are all part of this pre-crisis picture.

At the other end of the continuum, are the potential life-changing or life-altering consequences of experiencing a crisis in life. These too can go on for significant periods of time after the crisis has ended. In fact, it may be possible to achieve even greater levels of functioning in life depending on how the current crisis was handled. How it was handled may well depend on the effectiveness of the intervener. If the intervener proves not only effective but also trustworthy, the sufferer may be willing to accept suggestions for additional assistance as needed to develop higher level life skills.

Crisis intervention is about management and not about resolution. Therapy may be a source of resolution of problems. Crisis intervention is about trying to find a way to manage what is being experienced so that the crisis' destructive influences are diminished.

It is important to note that the goal of crisis intervention is extremely limited and short term. As mentioned above, higher levels of functioning are possible. However, the goal of the crisis intervener when assisting a sufferer in crisis is to return that sufferer to their own level of pre-crisis functioning. No more, no less. If the intervener accomplishes this, the goals of crisis intervention have been met. What may happen subsequently is a bonus. While a pre- and post-crisis functioning timeline may be measured in days or weeks or years, the time needed for effective crisis intervention is measured in seconds or minutes only. Any additional time you may get is a bonus for you as the intervener as well. (See Figure 1.2, page 4.)

FIGURE 1.6 – EFFECTIVE CRISIS AND DISASTER INTERVENTION
To remain helpful, we must remain effective.

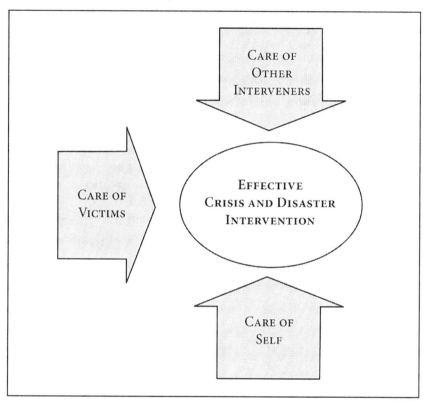

Crisis interveners have been compared to emergency room medical personnel in that their effective reactions, timing, and utilization of resources must be immediate and sure. If a counselor makes an error in a regular weekly session, they may be able to correct the error by phone or in person at the next session. On the other hand, the crisis intervener, like their emergency room counterparts, may have only one bite at the apple as it were. They may have one quick opportunity to be effective and failing that no other opportunity to try again. What the intervener does must be correct the first time without dependence on the possibility of a do-over. This may be why not all who want to can actually be crisis interveners; just as some may not be able to work in an emergency room although comfortable and competent in other professional settings.

A Final Note

Crises are by definition unexpected, sudden, and arbitrary. They are time sensitive and time specific. All crises end regardless of what an intervener may or may not do. The real question is where the crisis will end if the intervener does nothing or is ineffective. Remember that stress in unusual proportions for that person is key to understanding crisis. Interveners must react and be effective within seconds or minutes to avert additional problems. While the goal of crisis management, not resolution, is to return the sufferer to their level of pre-crisis functioning, greater gains for that sufferer may be possible depending on the credibility of the intervener and the effectiveness of the intervention. Crisis intervention or Emotional First Aid is comparable to physical first aid and must be administered with the same skill and alacrity. Never forget that knowing when to stay out is just as important to the intervener as knowing when to act.

Chapter 2

What to Do and How to Do It: Heeding the need for speed

**Remember and never forget:
Respond now.**

Figure 2.1 Crisis Intervention Model for Response
(Greenstone and Leviton, 1982)

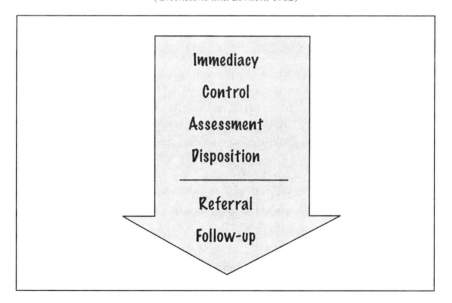

Immediacy

Control

Assessment

Disposition

Referral

Follow-up

This model is made up of only six words. That is no accident. When called upon to intervene in a crisis, the less one has to remember the better one's overall response will be. It could be argued that only the first four are absolutely necessary to be committed to memory. Referral and follow-up are usually not of the same urgency as the first four areas. If you get them in the correct order: Immediacy, Control, Assessment and Disposition, and if you follow the order, you will be involved and effective. This is true regardless of when you are called upon to respond. Crises do not always occur when it is convenient for us as interveners. In fact, most of the time they occur at the most inconvenient times or when we are most tired or at our lowest. Because of this, the four ingrained words of this model will likely click-in even before you are fully aware that they have engaged. Sometimes referred to as "auto-pilot," its importance should never be underestimated in our work.

Immediacy refers to the need to act immediately after having identified a person in crisis. This sets the battle rhythm for Crisis Intervention. If the intervener is going to react, the intervener must do it now. There is no time to read up on the proper procedures. The intervener must know what to do and do it just as emergency medical personnel must first attend to life threatening conditions such as bleeding, breathing, circulation, or poisoning. Persons in crisis may bleed emotionally and the end result of non-intervention can be just as devastating as ignoring arterial bleeding. We cannot see the emotional bleeding but we must know that it exists nonetheless and react as though it were so. If you are going to get involved, get involved when the crisis victim is encountered.

Control refers to the need to establish structure for the sufferer where little or none exists. A person in crisis is out-of-control. Accurately put, a person in crisis is out-of-structure. The way in which a crisis occurs in a person's life, the unusual stress present at the time, and the relative inability of the victim to cope with life as he or she can in non-crisis times testifies to the notion of being out-of-structure. This concept is much more descriptive than others used during these times. The job of the intervener after encountering the person in crisis is to provide the structure that may be lacking. The responder must provide this emotionally and may do this physically as well; whatever is needed when it is needed. To say to a mental health professional involved in a psychotherapeutic relationship that they must act as a crutch to a patient might be met with resistance. In a crisis, however, this is just part of the job. An intervener never takes control of a sufferer's life for one second longer than it is absolutely necessary to allow the victim to regain self-control. This time may be measured in minutes and seconds; maybe longer at certain times. As soon as control can be returned to the victim, Crisis Intervention directs that this control be returned. However, until that earliest moment, the intervener may have to be in control of the sufferer's life. The way that such control is portrayed will be dependent on the need of the victim and on the intervention style of the responder. Not every responder will be comfortable providing the needed structure in the same way.

Taking control of another person's life when he or she may not be able to rely on or determine self-structure may include making immediate decisions. Such decisions may have to do with safety issues, environmental issues, medical, and psychological issues. Additionally, physical control may be needed to move the victim out of harm's way or just to provide someone to physically lean on during the early stages of the crisis. The intervener is there to provide whatever is needed and responsive to the situation at hand. Control is an important issue for all interveners to study and understand. If the victim feels no sense of structure, little else will be accomplished by the crisis intervener. It is the structure in one's life that allows other adaptive behaviors to return and resiliency to be activated at its fullest. While control may not be the first choice of the therapist, it must be accomplished by the crisis intervener if the intervention is to continue. Skipping this stage will hinder the forthcoming stages of assessment and disposition. Also, it may reduce the likelihood that a needed referral will be accepted by the victim.

Assessment is the stage that is most often skipped by interveners overly zealous about doing something to or for the victim. It can never be avoided, although the way it is done may be modified in order to adapt effectively to particular situations. Assessments are to be limited in scope. Under crisis conditions, a detailed clinical history is much too much for conditions. An immediate history focusing on what happened within the previous few minutes to a few hours may be all that is needed. This is enough to get the intervention started and to make initial decisions about what to do to help the sufferer. If there was not time initially to gather the needed information, the intervener may have to go ahead and make some decisions concerning the sufferer. Always feel free to go back and continue to gather information when possible and prudent. Just because you do not have all of the history you need is no reason not to respond to the emerging situation, for instance, to get the victim out of harm's way. On the other hand, there is no reason not to continue the assessment after these first steps are taken. The better the assessment, the better the care of the victim will be. While the model presented here is generally to be followed as outlined, it should be remembered that earlier stages of the model may need to be revisited as the intervention continues. The areas of immediacy and control may need to be continually reevaluated. Additional assessment information may need to be gathered. All of this moves us to the next step of providing specific care to the victim or victims encountered.

Disposition refers to making decisions about what you will do to assist the sufferer. We know that either removing the victim from the situation or removing the situation from the victim will often stem the immediate crisis and lower stress. Crisis intervention dictates that whatever is done be effective and be the least that must be done to afford relief. No more; no less. Crisis intervention is not psychotherapy or counseling. It is not crisis counseling. The short-term, goal-limited, immediate, emotional first aid response to an out-of-structure victim is to provide the necessary structure and return the victim to pre-crisis levels of functioning. (See Figure 1.1, pg. 2) The other modalities mentioned above may or may not be needed subsequently. The better done the initial intervention, the less likely the other modalities will be needed later. However, at this point they should never be confused or improperly used. It is most important that we understand what it is we are doing and do it effectively. Little else matters here.

Referral. Proper referral or transfer to additional care can make or break your intervention and reduce the effectiveness of all of the work you have done to that point. The time to plan your referrals is now. What do you have available to you and thereby the victim? Find out early. In day-to-day intervention in crises, know what referral resources are available and functioning within your area of operations. Who do they accept and how should the referral be made. Do they accept persons in crisis? What related training do their personnel possess? Referrals taken from the telephone book are often fraught with problems and uncertainties that neither you nor the victim need to encounter. If you have done your homework in the area ahead of time, many referral problems can be avoided. When you arrive on the scene of a disaster where you will be working with crisis victims, find out early what referral sources are available to you within those circumstances. Do not expect the usual services that you might find in non-disaster times. How you do this will make such a transfer the best it can be under the circumstances and give the sufferer the best chance of receiving what they need. Start thinking about referral and how best to do this as you are planning for deployment. Do not find yourself short in this area. You may be *ready* to respond to the crisis of others, but are you *prepared* to respond?

Follow-up is usually a luxury during and after Crisis Intervention. This may be especially true when doing disaster crisis management. There will often be too many to follow and more work than you can handle as you do everything else required of you. You will want to do some follow-up

FIG. 2.2 – CRISIS CASUALTY RESPONSE CHART
Print this page and keep it in the front of your Crisis Intervention Notebook.

While victim is still involved	Care after removal of victim from crisis situation	Evacuation: Medivac vs. Emotional First Aid Evacuation
Expect that a crisis victim may stay involved within the crisis situation…e.g. continue to clear rubble from their destroyed house.	Assess altered mental status.	Specify best route in to location.
Work alongside the crisis victim as needed.	Perform physical first aid as needed.	Radio – specify channels or frequencies.
Keep self out of harm's way.	Airway establishment.	Specify number of patients to be evacuated and precedence.
Keep victim from additional or greater stress if possible.	Breathing checked.	Medical.
Expect the sufferer's stress level may increase.	Bleeding stopped.	Immediate.
Attend to minor physical wounds.	Splint broken bones.	Delayed.
Prevent additional physical wounds.	Communicate with victim.	Minor.
Stop any life threatening behavior.	Cardiopulmonary resuscitation as needed.	Extreme.
Maintain appropriate communication with sufferers.	Check wounds.	Specify equipment needed.
Explain your actions to the sufferer.	Get victim to medical clearing as soon as possible as needed.	Specify how many victims are ambulatory.
Reassure realistically.	The "ABC's" of Emotional First Aid: Begin Emotional First Aid immediately.	Specify how many victims are on litters.
Remove victim from crisis situation if additional emotional or physical injury may occur.	A = Assessment and control B = Begin emotional first aid C = Clear sufferer to definitive care	Describe security at pick-up site and inform them of the pending arrival of evacuation personnel and vehicles.
Evacuate as appropriate to definitive care.	Assessment and control— Begin Emotional First Aid— Clear to care	Describe the method of marking the pick-up site.
Stay hydrated.	Fluids as needed.	Describe the contamination, if any.
Help victim stay hydrated.	Reassure victims realistically.	None.
Other concerns, Notes, Lists.		Emotional First Aid only.
		Nuclear.
		Biological.
		Chemical.

as you find the time to do so. If you can, do it. If not, understand that the situation may make follow-up difficult if not impossible at times. Even in day-to-day crisis intervention, follow-up with victims may not always be possible. Additionally, remember that any attempts to check on victims with whom you have had contact should not interfere with the additional, advanced or definitive care that they may be receiving.

A Final Note

Disaster Crisis Intervention in a nutshell:

- Effective crisis intervention can reduce the need for counseling or therapy later on.
- Interveners have a "Duty to Normalize."
- The goal for survivors is to find a way to get past the traumatic events, not to get over them.
- Keep the victim hydrated.

See Hydration Chart in Appendix A, page 110.

Chapter 3

Crisis Triage: Attending to those who can benefit the most

**Remember and never forget:
Those who can survive must survive.**

Triage can be tricky. This is true especially if you don't know what you are supposed to do and / or how to do it. If you don't know what it is and why it is important, you may waste a lot of valuable time that you really do not have to spare and deplete your resources.

During a disaster situation involving multiple victims, everyone seems to want a piece of you as the intervener or designated mental health worker. When they find out what you do, they may think that you can solve their problems for them or may have some special insights on which they can rely. While this is not so in most cases, some victims are looking for the struc-

FIGURE 3.1 – What Crisis Interveners Do

- Question sufferer cogently.
- Observe victim keenly.
- Listen carefully to sufferer.
- Think deeply about the victim's problems.
- Think as a crisis intervener.
- Statistics cannot substitute for the sufferer before you.
- Victims can help interveners think.

Figure. 3.2 – Crisis Intervention
and Disaster Crisis Intervention

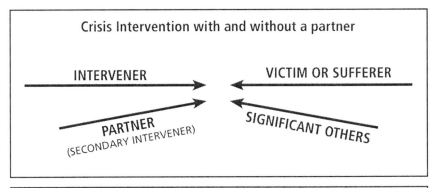

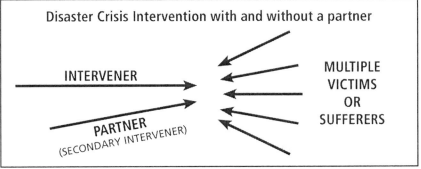

ture in their life that they feel helpless to provide for themselves. This is an intervener trap that can be limiting to your ability to provide effective care.

An example is a call made to this author from a relatively new counselor who had been asked by her local professional association to respond to the victims of Hurricane Katrina. She and a small number of colleagues dutifully reported to the shelter housing the victims of the storm. They spent at least a shift at the shelter and left. During the time at the shelter, these uninitiated were beset by those in great need of assistance. Unlike their counseling offices, the victims of the disaster were all around them, seeking whatever help they could get. The experience was reported as daunting at the very least. This relatively new counselor, with many hours of patient contact in her office, reported that her several colleagues would not return for another shift at the shelter and that she was evaluating whether or not she would return also. Hence the call. She had never experienced the onslaught of sufferers all at one time as she encountered at the shelter. Men and women; children of all ages, parents with multiple concerns, those needing help in all shapes and sizes; with little overall leadership for the mental health contingent. She reported, "Everyone seemed to want something from me." She was overwhelmed and did not want to be exposed to that again. She was unprepared for what she was asked to do.

In the conversation with her, some of the direction mentioned above was given to her. She was told that if she returned to:

1. Find a specific issue or area in which she felt that she could be most helpful.

2. Do what was realistically possible with the victims directly in front of her rather than spreading herself too thin over the multiple sufferers in front of her.

3. Be realistic about her capabilities and perform accordingly regardless of anything else.

4. Understand that this type of work cannot be done by just anyone.

Special training and preparation is vital to effective functioning in this venue. She was thrown into the mix without any training whatsoever, and was relying on the old assumption that a good counselor automatically makes a good crisis intervener. This is just not so. Not returning to the shelter should be an acceptable option for her. If she did return, she must be armed with the knowledge of what it means to be effective in those circumstances.

The end of this story is an interesting one. She did return to the shelter. None of her colleagues did. She called again and this time the report was different. She found an area of need that she could handle and attended to it directly and efficiently. She found that she responded well to the children of this disaster and put her efforts to work there. In the shelter, a child care play area was established. She was ready for this and put her skills to good use. Whether or not she will become a disaster responder is yet to be seen. She knows what she will be getting herself into or at least what she is avoiding; either is okay with her. (Personal Communication, Anonymous, September 2005).

Effective crisis interveners cannot, and will not, give away a piece of who they are to everyone that they encounter. You will run out of "pieces" quickly and decrease your overall effectiveness. We know this in the counseling or psychotherapy session. The disaster environment is just too intense for many and interveners may over identify with the seemingly unending line of sufferers. Take on what you can realistically handle, and do your work effectively with them. If you can, be selective about those with whom you will intervene.

Respond to those who you believe that you can assist best. Do not try to be all things to all people and remember that a major goal of Crisis Intervention is to return control back to the victim as soon as possible. While we may act as a crutch initially, control must go back to the sufferer at the earliest possible point when they might be able to accept it. The intervener must not retain control of a victim's life any longer than absolutely necessary. To do so weakens the sufferer's ability to bounce back from their crisis.

Essentially, to triage is to sort. In multiple victim and disaster situations, it is a way of determining who needs help, what kind of help they need, and the likelihood of survival. Once this is done, the priority for attention and treatment is assigned.

FIGURE. 3.3 – CRISIS INTERVENTION TRIAGE SYSTEM.

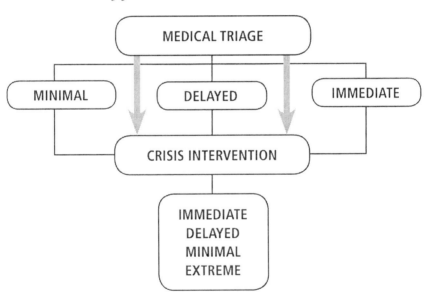

Use your triage skills to assist you and the victims encountered. Adults, kids, parents, grandparents, men, women, teenagers, and anyone else you may encounter need to be given the most appropriate care. Not necessarily the maximum care or the resource-depleting care, but that care that takes into account what the capabilities of both the intervener and the victims actually are in the specific situation in which you find yourself. Intervention with a single victim is different than intervention with multiple presentations all at the same time. Resources are always an issue. If you have them, no problem. If not, they have to be parceled out so that those who can benefit most are immediately assisted. As triage is an ongoing, rather than one-time process, those not identified initially for immediate care may be moved into that category later. Triage must be done continually throughout the crisis or disaster. Remember that you will probably never get to everyone in need. Such is the nature of the beast. It is advised that all interveners work with a partner throughout the interventions. Having someone at your side has an immediate psychological effect on the primary intervener as well as providing another person to handle other issues as they present. Primary and secondary interveners should take care of each other before, during and after the interventions and provide a source for debriefing each other.

Disaster and crisis situations dictate that available care be allocated first to those sufferers who can benefit from such care, and have the best likelihood of survival considering the often limited resources available at the time. A triage system for disaster mental health and crisis intervention must be a simple process that can be accomplished with limited training and performed quickly. It should be done without sacrificing the dignity of the victim while at the same time making critical decisions about who will get scarce care and who will have to wait or get no medical or psychological care at all. It is a basic tenet of psychological triage that it be performed on victims who have received needed medical care or who may have been screened medically and require no medical care.

This system has been developed in a way similar to triage systems used in emergency medicine. It is most closely linked to the M.A.S.S. Triage System promulgated by the National Disaster Life Support Foundations and American Medical Association in its Basic and Advanced Disaster Life Support courses. (2006, 2007.)

The Disaster Crisis Intervention Triage System should be used by:

A. Experienced disaster mental health and Crisis Intervention personnel in the course of their work with traumatized victims of disaster.

B. Mental health workers less familiar with disaster Crisis Intervention techniques but desiring to assist.

C. Inexperienced volunteers who receive "Just-in-time" training in the Disaster Crisis Intervention Triage System.

FIGURE 3.4 – TRIAGE CARD, PART 1, SIDE 1
To be used and retained by triage intervener.

Name		Last 4 SS#
4 – EXTREME (BLACK) Complete emotional shutdown; Severe mental illness		
To: CARE	Location:	Behavioral Health
1 – IMMEDIATE (RED) Serious crisis that requires and will respond to STAT intervention		
To: CRISIS INTERVENTION	Location:	Behavioral Health
2 – DELAYED (YELLOW) Experiencing crisis but can wait until IMMEDIATE are seen		
To: GROUP	Location:	Behavioral Health
3 – MINIMAL (GREEN) Experiencing post trauma stress, but with some intact coping skills		
To: REST AREA or ASSIST __R __A	Location:	Behavioral Health

FIGURE 3.4 – TRIAGE CARD, PART 1, SIDE 2

Basic Overview of the Four Levels of Triage

The Disaster Crisis Intervention Triage System presented here consists of four levels of triage. This is similar to many of the emergency medical triage systems.

MINIMAL LEVEL

Few indicators of crisis. Upset and /or experiencing effects of psychosocial trauma with few or no indicators of crisis, as indicated by some of the following:
1. Coherent thought processes.
2. Able to make personal care decisions.
3. Upset or crying but obviously in control of self.
4. Able and willing to discuss experience.
5. No violent acting out behavior.
6. May want to help others.
7. Re-triage may be needed.

IMMEDIATE LEVEL

Must be seen and attended to now! In crisis as indicated by some of the following:
1. Becoming more and more depressed.
2. Out-of-structure (control issues).
3. Acting out behavior.
4. Difficulty following instructions.
5. Poor decision making.
6. Yelling and screaming.

DELAYED LEVEL

Can wait. Must be re-triaged. Very upset but obviously coping to some degree as indicated by some of the following:
1. Some withdrawal.
2. Some confusion.
3. No acting out behavior.
4. Intact decision making.
5. Expression of concerns and desire to talk to someone.

EXTREME LEVEL

Return to these only when others are assisted. May need to re-triage later as time and resources permit. These will require long-term support or psychotherapy and are not likely to respond to Crisis Intervention techniques as indicated by some of, but not limited to, the following:
1. Chronic mental illness without appropriate medications.
2. Totally unresponsive to inquiries.
3. Communication shut-down.
4. Unable to do anything for self.
5. Custodial care probably required.

FIGURE 3.5 – TRIAGE CARD, PART 2
To be attached to the crisis victim.

Name	Last 4 SS#

4 – EXTREME (BLACK)

To: CARE	Location:	Behavioral Health

1 – IMMEDIATE (RED)

To: CRISIS INTERVENTION	Location:	Behavioral Health

2 – DELAYED (YELLOW)

To: GROUP	Location:	Behavioral Health

3 – MINIMAL (GREEN)

To: REST AREA or ASSIST __R __A	Location:	Behavioral Health

Characteristics of Each Psychological Level – Another Look

1. IMMEDIATE – treat now. They can benefit instantly from immediate Crisis Intervention. This is what they look like:

> **Attitude and General Behavior** — Extremely upset, hyperactive, defiant, angry, overwhelmed, preoccupied, mistrustful, scared, limited self-control.

> **Mental Activity** — Self-absorbed, illogical, irrelevant, difficulty expressing complete thoughts, generally coherent.

> **Emotional Reactions** — Euphoric or depressed, apprehension, fear, emotions easily aroused or expressed, generally appropriate affect.

> **Thoughts** — Some trouble forming clear thoughts, fearful, shut down.

> **Orientation** — Clear sensorium.

> **Fund of General Knowledge** — Appropriate to age and education, some production difficulties at the outset.

> **Suicidality** — Thoughts may be present.

> **Insight** — Limited.

2. DELAYED – treat as soon as possible. They can wait awhile although best in a group. These can benefit from Crisis Intervention, but are not suffering to the same extent as the immediates. This is what they look like:

> **Attitude and General Behavior** — Upset, basically in control of self, mild mistrust, talkative, may make light, nervous giggle.

> **Mental Activity** — Accessible, worried, concerned about situation and that of others, compliant.

> **Emotional Reactions** — Appropriate to the situation, anxiety, moderate fear, moderate depression.

> **Thoughts** — May have difficulty accessing clear thoughts, may catastrophize, concern about others, wants to help self and others, may intellectualize situation and their response, stream of thoughts may be less than adequate to maintain a conversation.

> **Orientation** — Sensorium clear in all three realms of time, person and place.

> **Fund of General Knowledge** — Appropriate to age and education.

Suicidality — May have some fleeting suicidal ideations, denies suicidal desires.

Insight — Some, but still limited, less limited than those in IMMEDIATE category.

3. MINIMAL — treat later. They can get along on their own for now. May not be in crisis, but could be headed in that direction. Probably will do fine with support and even with utilization as a volunteer to assist you in helping or monitoring others. Just because they look okay initially, does not mean that they might not experience crisis later. Pay attention to this group but put them to work if they are willing. If not, check on them occasionally as resources allow. This is what they look like:

Attitude and General Behavior — Presents well, could appear calm or preoccupied but in control of self, compliant and cooperative, responsive to inquiries, positive attitude.

Mental Activity — Accessible, coherent and relevant, alert and appropriately talkative.

Emotional Reactions — Appropriate affect, mild depression, mild fear, some anxiety, emotionally stable.

Thoughts — Within normal limits, relates to others easily, engages in conversation and is easily understood, maintains appropriate stream of thoughts.

Orientation — Well oriented in all spheres.

Fund of General Knowledge — Appropriate.

Suicidality — No suicidal ideation.

Insight — Appropriate to age, education and current experience.

4. EXTREME — Will not benefit from the help available at this time or requires more assistance than resources allow. Are so mentally disturbed that attempts to help them would require hours of time and personnel needed elsewhere, and the benefit to the patient would be minimal or non-existent. Attempts to treat these cases would occur after all of the above groups have been helped. This is what they look like:

Attitude and General Behavior — Disheveled and untidy, limited cooperation, mistrustful, suspicious, antagonistic, motor retardation or hyperactivity, perseveration.

Mental Activity — Self-absorbed or inaccessible, circumstantial, flight of ideas, underproductive, mute, irrelevant, incoherent, illogical, blocking.

Emotional Reactions — Elation, exhilaration, depression, emotional instability, incongruity of thought content, ambivalence, emotional deterioration.

Thoughts — Delusions, hallucinations, paranoid ideations, grandiose ideas, autistic thinking, unreal ideas.

Orientation — Limited orientation in three spheres: Person, place and time.

Fund of General Knowledge — May be appropriate.

Suicidality — Suicidal ideations may be present, prior suicidal behavior, plan of suicide clear, means of suicide clear.

Insight — May be non-existent.

Ask about a previous diagnosis or treatment and medications related to mental health problems. Most likely there will be positive responses to at least some of these inquiries.

NB: People in crisis could appear mentally ill and those who are mentally ill could be in crisis. Differentiation is crucial. Generally, if a person in crisis is removed from the source of the crisis, or if the crisis situation is removed from the person in crisis, the crisis will subside substantially. This is not true for a person who is mentally ill. The mental illness may be exacerbated or diminished by removal, but the mental illness continues.

Questions or Observations Needed to Complete the Triage Process

1. Please give me your attention so that we can get you the help you need. If you need medical treatment have you received it? (If no, refer to medical triage. Escort as needed and as possible.

2. Those who need immediate medical care or medications, please move over here so that we can get you the care you need.

3. Look for: very distraught, screaming and yelling. Out-of-control or out-of-structure. Panic, unable to care for self effectively, illogical thinking, reacting to the disaster even though currently safe.

4. Incoherent speech. If no, go to Number 6.
   a. If yes, separate to alternate location. Tag IMMEDIATE.

   b. Tell them "Please come with us. We are going to help you now."

5. Not screaming or yelling, but showing 1000 yard stare, crying, sobbing, wandering, autism, confusion. (No). If yes, these are DELAYED. Keep this group together and monitor. Reassure as a group.

6. Keep families together if at all possible.

7. Provide needed information about the situation and resources to the remaining group.

8. Remaining group accepts information as helpful. If yes, with limited symptomology, these are MINIMAL.

9. Enlist the aid of those willing MINIMALs to assist with other patients. Train them to triage as needed. Use them to help in other needed areas as their abilities and talents allow.

10. If no to question number 8, information is not accepted as helpful and displayed are symptoms of mental illness or chronic mental disabilities, they are EXTREME. Place away from others and put a custodial monitor in place.

11. DELAYED becomes the next IMMEDIATE after IMMEDIATE are helped.

12. MINIMALs become IMMEDIATE after the DELAYED are helped.

13. The EXTREME become the IMMEDIATE after all others have been helped and if resources are still available. They may require custodial care during this time.

14. Triage is an ongoing process that must be done continually. It is not a onetime procedure. Ongoing triage may change the grouping originally established.

15. Those with Medically Unexplained Symptoms (MUPS): These are sometimes inappropriately called the "Worried well." These individuals should be taken seriously and guided toward an area where they can associate with other MUPS and have someone with whom they may speak within that area. Individuals with MUPS are

suffering as are others who are victims of a disaster. They have a right to be worried and they have developed symptoms that may need to be addressed either medically or psychologically. Pay due attention to this group. Do not disregard them as non-sufferers. That would be a mistake.

A Final Note

This system of triage continues to be tested, revised and studied. It should be treated accordingly and improved upon by those using it. There are other systems of triage available. Some are better than others and more or less confusing and complicated. The key is simplicity and specificity. This triage system involves the use of two triage cards. The two cards replace the single card procedure often seen. The purpose of the two cards is that the victim / sufferer card has nothing on it concerning the condition of the victim. This was done thoughtfully in order to avoid creating additional problems or concerns for the victim who may have the opportunity to read their own card. However, the card does direct them to appropriate care and care locations within the situation. Whatever is utilized in the field to document triage results should bear this special need in mind. (Some of the above material was revised and adapted from Greenstone, 2008.) Please refer to the variety of intake forms in Appendix A.

Chapter 4

Intervener Survival: Indispensable Self-Care

Remember and never forget: Effective force protection must be in place if effective victim care is to happen.

There is a myth out there that if one is a mental health provider that taking time for care of self is less important than to the average, non-mental health worker. We have special knowledge and abilities and therefore do not need to indulge ourselves to take care of our needs. Certainly, this is not the case. There is a relationship between the effectiveness of an intervener and the degree to which that intervener has taken time to prepare for the intervention, has taken time to deal with personal issues related to the crisis situation, has given themselves time to recover from the effects of doing the intervention, and has sought help for themselves as realistically needed. There is a difference between being ready to serve and being prepared to serve. We are better at what we do if we take care of ourselves first and foremost.

In order to be helpful, we must remain effective. How we accomplish this is related to how we take care of ourselves. Many of us were raised to believe that we must give all to others before we give to ourselves. This just does not work. Giving to ourselves first will go a long way to insure that what we give to others is the best that it can be based on our skills and training. Effective Crisis Intervention should not expect the victims to return the care given to them. We do what we do because we have our life together before we attempt to help others achieve the same. It seems to work that way in actual practice. Take time to look at this. It may not be easy, but it is important that you do it. NB: See Force Protection references in Appendix C. Advance Directive for Crisis Interveners can be found on page 166.

FIGURE 1.6. EFFECTIVE CRISIS AND DISASTER INTERVENTION
To remain helpful, we must remain effective.

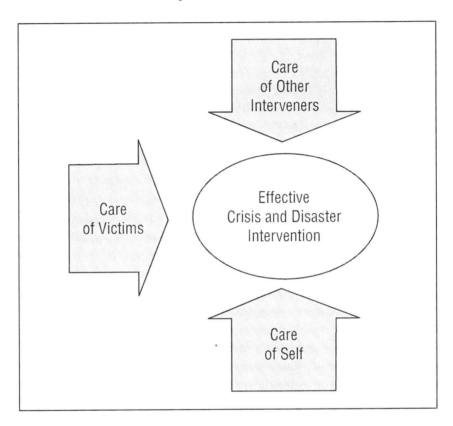

Five Steps to Total Relaxation and Reduction of Tension

These five steps can be used almost anywhere and at any time. They were adapted from some of the work done in this field by Dr. Edward S. Rosenbluh. During total relaxation, your mind remains alert. As long as you do not do the steps for longer than twenty minutes, you are not likely to fall asleep. When you are finished, you will feel relaxed and fresh. Those skilled at relaxing even talk of a "natural high" produced without drugs.

When time or circumstances do not permit following the whole program, you may do parts of it. It can be done with your eyes open or shut. It can be done for short periods of time. It can even be done in a meeting, as a passenger in a car, during breaks or down-time, and during other appropriate or private times. You will feel more refreshed and alert even after a short session than if you had remained tense the entire time.

Step One: Sit or lie in a comfortable position. Allow the weight of all parts of your body to be supported. Lean your head forward if sitting, or back if lying down.

Step Two: Close your eyes and relax all parts of your body. Feel your feet getting heavy and relaxed, then your ankles, knees, hips, mid-section, hand, arms, shoulders, neck, jaw, eyes, forehead, and even your tongue. Feel each part of your body, in succession, starting with your feet, become heavy, relaxed and comfortable.

Step Three: Begin to concentrate on your breathing. Observe it with your mind as it slowly goes in and out. During each exhale, say the word, "One," to yourself. It's easier that it seems: Inhale, exhale, "One," inhale, exhale, "One," etc.

Step Four: The word "One" will help keep meaningful thoughts from your mind. Do not worry if fleeting thoughts come in and out of focus. Concentrate on breathing and on "One."

Step Five: Continue for 20 minutes. Do this once in the morning and once in the evening, as needed and as possible or at any time you feel tense. You may check the clock periodically. Because of digestion, which might interfere, it would be best to avoid total relaxation for about two hours after eating. If you feel your hands getting warmer, this is okay. Such sensations often accompany total relaxation. Sometimes, it even helps to think about your hands and arms getting warmer after Step Two. (Greenstone, 2008).

High stress levels, personal frustration, and inadequate coping skills have major personal, team, organizational, and social costs. Stress is not a mental illness. Rather, it is a part of everyday living. Each of us is potentially vulnerable to the problem of unusual stress and not enough coping ability. No one can underestimate the importance of managing stress during crisis situations, interventions and disaster work.

Taking care of oneself does not guarantee effective Crisis Intervention; it enhances the possibility of successful intervention.

Signs and Symptoms of Stress and Burnout

1. High resistance to doing your job
2. A pervasive sense of failure, as indicated by such expressions as "I can't do enough"; "I can't get it right"; "I'm no good anymore."
3. Anger and resentment.
4. Guilt and blame. These might be expressed by such expressions as, "No matter how many hours I work, I never finish and I feel guilty about leaving. I'm in a 'no-win' situation."
5. Discouragement and indifference.
6. Negativism.
7. Isolation and withdrawal.
8. Feelings of tiredness and exhaustion.
9. Frequent clock watching.
10. Extreme fatigue.
11. Loss of positive feelings.
12. Postponement of victim contacts.
13. Inability to concentrate or listen to information.
14. Feelings of immobilization.
15. Cynicism toward victims, co-workers, or the world in general.
16. Sleep disorders, including difficulty either in falling asleep or in staying asleep, or sleeping an adequate amount but not feeling rested upon waking. These disorders occur regularly over an extended period.
17. Self-preoccupation.
18. Increased need of behavior-control measures, such as tranquilizers.
19. Frequent colds and flu.
20. Frequent headaches and gastrointestinal disturbances.
21. Rigidity in thinking and resistance to change.
22. Suspicion and paranoia.
23. Excessive drug use.
24. Marital and family conflict; new or continuing due to your deployment or activation.
25. Free-floating anxiety, evidenced by such expressions as, "I am constantly worried and anxious, but I can't pinpoint what I'm upset about."
26. Tunnel vision: as stress increases, perception of available options narrows.
27. A sense of increasing helplessness.
28. Fear that "It won't get better."
29. Fear of losing control.
30. High absenteeism or not showing up for assignments.

Intervener and victim alike are subject to stressors, and both can become incapacitated as a result of unmanaged stress.

We must recognize that a person in crisis cannot provide effective assistance to another person who is also in crisis. Therefore, it is a logical step to incorporate into our Crisis Intervention training an ongoing discussion of the importance of self-awareness, self-protection, proper nutrition, time to play, personal stress management and wellness as one prepares to be an intervener. The discussion continues to be about humor and balance, preparation and seeking clarity in one's professional and personal life. It is about taking responsibility for being a responsible intervener.

Teachable Moments in Crisis Intervention

As explained earlier, the basic role of the intervener or disaster responder is to effectively diffuse a potentially disastrous situation and to help the sufferer to return to his or her level of pre-crisis functioning. Be alert to the potential for teachable moments. These possibilities can occur during the assessment, the disposition and the referral phases. No lectures. No biased propaganda. Use personal opinions sparingly, if at all. Personal opinions should be labeled as such. Use well-placed questions to draw out the sufferer's own ideas and options for managing the problem. Use appropriate encouragers, model active listening, provide accurate information, recognize the moment when a "light bulb" seems to come on. That is a teachable moment.

Keep Stress Within Tolerable Limits

The following are suggestions for keeping stress within tolerable limits:

1. Eliminate stressor foods from your diet. Nutritional stress can be as debilitating as emotional stress.
2. Get enough sleep and rest.
3. Exercise regularly and appropriately for your age and fitness level.
4. Be realistic about the givens of your world. Work within the reality of "what is" today.
5. Realistically assess what you are able to do in your particular situation.
6. Schedule time for fun. Allow time each day to experience good feelings. Even a little time away from the disaster front or front lines is recommended.

(Continued on the next page)

(Continued from previous page)

7. Schedule regular recreation or vacation time. The quantity of time spent is not important; the quality of time spent in recreation is a key to stress reduction.

8. Be sure you receive your minimum daily requirement of positive nurturing.

9. Set realistic goals in all areas of your endeavors and involvements.

10. Consider the following carefully:

    a. Everything I do is the result of a choice I make.

    b. Every choice I make benefits me positively in some way even though I may not know what the benefit is at the moment.

    c. I have inside me everything I need and all the tools I need to guide my life successfully.

    d. I can choose to gain greater self-awareness.

    e. I am responsible for 100% of my life.

    f. The degree to which others control my life is the degree to which I allow them to control it.

    g. I cannot easily change my feelings, but I can always change my behavior.

    h. Any problem I experience in my life is a problem that I have created for myself.

    i. If I choose to continue creating a particular problem for myself, I do it because:

        (1) I receive some pleasure or unacknowledged benefit or payoff for continuing the problem, or

        (2) I can avoid greater or more fearful problems by perpetuating the current problem. In other words, if I solve the current problem, I am afraid the greater problem will occur.

11. Develop interests outside of your specialized field.

12. Identify what is important to you.

13. Have a "Battle Buddy." Find someone to talk to. Ask them to just listen to you and to be there for you and you will do the same for them.

14. Surround yourself with people who have a positive attitude.

15. Find an ongoing support system to access as needed both in the field and out.

16. Be aware of situations that may trigger an unresolved issue.

17. Recognize the effect that the sufferer's pain has on you.

18. Acknowledge the feelings that you have and allow them to be whatever they are.

19. Recognize that working harder, faster, longer, or punishing your body will not relieve the pain or lessen the stress.

20. Recognize that neglecting your own needs, interests and health will eventually create more pain and problems for you, and lessen your effectiveness.

21. Slot into your appointment book a time for yourself. This does not require a lengthy period of time. It does need to be doable. Be creative.

Dr. Leviton's 48 Steps to Pro-Active Management for Reducing Stress

(Greenstone and Leviton, 2011)

Early avoidance of stress and those things that exacerbate it is a good place to start for any intervener. Pay attention to what follows and utilize the information as you can. Be clear in preparing a job description.

1. Be clear in delegating responsibility.

2. Be clear in assigning tasks.

3. Be realistic in assigning responsibilities.

4. Be realistic about expectations.

5. See the big picture. Every decision has an impact and a consequence. Nothing operates in a vacuum.

6. Respond. Don't react.

7. Plan and then act.

8. Be consistent. Don't keep changing the rules. When others are unclear about policy and function, their level of stress and anxiety escalates. They may feel out of structure. Feeling left without a mechanism for relief only potentiates crisis.

9. Be reliable. Act reliably. Ensure that your actions match your words.

10. Create an environment that is orderly and efficient.

11. Be explicit in setting policy. Apply the policy in an even handed manner.

(Continued on the next page)

(Continued from previous page)

12. Provide support, structure, and information to those who need it.

13. Encourage and place a value on creativity and innovation.

14. Communicate in a timely, appropriate, accurate manner.

15. Be accessible. When and how can you be reached?

16. To be trusted, you must be honest.

17. Know what is going on within your area of responsibility.

18. Be aware of your surroundings. You will gain valuable information about how things are going by using your sensing mechanisms.

19. Encourage input. It is all right not to have all the answers. Involving others increases the sense of satisfaction, commitment and dedication for all concerned.

20. Give directions as needed and as appropriate.

21. Give feedback on a timely schedule.

22. Be fair. Act fairly despite personal biases.

23. Encourage professional development.

24. Create a safe environment. This includes both physical and emotional safety. Be clear that harassment of any nature will not be tolerated. Take necessary actions immediately if violations of the policy occur.

25. Create a supportive and non-defensive climate.

26. Identify potential stressors in your work environment.

27. Recognize symptoms of stress in yourself and others.

28. Be aware of the relationship of unmanaged stress to crisis.

29. Understand the relationship of stress/crisis/burnout.

30. Decide how to respond to the stress that you are experiencing, the signs of stress that others may be exhibiting and the potential stressors that you observed.

31. Recognize the cost of burnout.

32. Recognize the benefit of effective intervention.

33. Accept personal responsibility for your feelings and your behavior.

34. Allow your feelings to be what they are.

35. Separate your feelings from your behavior. You cannot always voluntarily change your feelings, but you can always voluntarily change your actions.

36. Be realistic about the givens of your world.

37. Realistically assess what you can do in your particular situation.

38. Set realistic goals in all areas of your life.

39. Get sufficient rest and sleep.

40. Eliminate stressor foods from your diet. Nutritional stress can be as debilitating as emotional stress.

41. Schedule time on your calendar for fun. Allow time each day to experience good feelings.

42. Schedule time each week on your calendar for dreaming, thinking, wandering, exploring and planning. Quiet time has special benefits.

43. Encourage peer networks of support among members.

44. Teach conflict resolution skills to those with whom you work.

45. Recognize that supervisor evaluation of performance should be a continuous process rather than an occasional event.

    a. Discuss the evaluation procedure in advance.

    b. Encourage self-evaluation.

    c. Keep the focus of the evaluation on performance.

    d. Review strengths and weaknesses, growth and stagnation. Be fair and clear.

    e. Focus on modifiable aspects of performance.

    f. Formulate the evaluations with some consistency. Apply the same standards in the same way to all who have approximately the same education and experience.

46. Recognize the necessity of humor even in difficult situations.

47. Be aware that you set the climate for your organization, team, etc.

48. Remember that most would like to feel a sense of commitment, challenge and some control in their assignments. (Greenstone and Leviton, 2011)

A Final Note

Take care of yourself if you expect to provide effective care to others. You come first. Your importance to disaster and crisis victims justifies this approach.

Chapter 5

Victim and Sufferer Survival: Helping to bounce back

Remember and never forget: Resiliency will out.

The effectiveness of Crisis Intervention is dependent on the resiliency of the victim; their mental toughness. This chapter's focus is on the victims / sufferers who may find themselves in a crisis or disaster situation. Responses of interveners or disaster responders are also referenced.

Most people have some level of resiliency. It would be difficult to get through daily life without it. The ability to bounce back from a crisis or a disaster may be something else altogether. As you saw in the Crisis Cube, (Figure 1.2, page 4) when stress makes it unlikely that you can continue to cope with life in the usual manner, crisis occurs. What we do to assist as crisis or disaster interveners is an important component of "bounce-back." Can we do some calming? What about insuring the safety of the victim? Keeping family members and / or friends together, or even keeping unrelated persons together, may help at least in the early hours. It has been said that "misery loves company." The key is to remember that those in misery only want the company of those who have experienced the same misery as they have experienced. Connections become very important. However, what the victims bring to the table during these trying times may well spell the difference between the success or failure of our attempts to help. A feeling of being hopeful or empowered may be at the top of the list of what is needed. Provide and encourage what you can and realize that you will be providing this, or looking for this, in multiple victims perhaps simultaneously.

Figure 5.1 below may be helpful in understanding the components of resiliency and recognizing them in the victims we encounter. In this way, we may be able to encourage such behavior in our sufferers. Trying to put components of resiliency in place where these components do not already exist will be less satisfying than capitalizing on what the victim is currently demonstrating.

FIGURE 5.1 – GREENSTONE'S 25

Resiliency equals:

1. Looking for benefits in encountered problems.
2. Adapting quickly to difficulties.
3. Feeling stronger in the midst of adversity.
4. Optimism. An optimistic outlook at all times.
5. Independence. Acting independently.
6. Expecting to overcome difficulties whenever and wherever met.
7. Personal durability.
8. Calmness through any storm.
9. Letting go of discouragement.
10. Staying focused.
11. Letting go of anger.
12. Intuition utilization. Trusting your feelings and your inklings.
13. Expression of feelings. Yours and others.
14. Curiousness. Creativity and seeking the truth.
15. Adaptiveness. Overcome and Prevail.
16. Willingness to learn.
17. Non-judgment of self and others.
18. Flexibility.
19. Listening well to others.
20. Anticipating problems.
21. Good self-esteem. Let the good in you always show.
22. Tolerance for ambiguity.
23. Avoidance of problems when possible.
24. Empathizing with others.
25. Self-confidence.

The Center for Disease Control lays out some guidelines for disaster and crisis responders that may be quite useful and applicable to crisis and disaster victims. The guidelines for victims include such things as:

1. Reminding sufferers to take breaks away from the main disaster area and to pace themselves in all activities. The disaster or crisis event may continue for a long time.

2. Take care of each other. Crisis victims should be encouraged to have a Battle Buddy.

3. Watch your Battle Buddy. Know where he or she is.

4. Talk with them as needed.

5. If they need to talk to you, be available.

6. Protect yourself and your partner from injury.

7. Point out hazards as you encounter them and remain aware of them.

8. Be willing to listen to the fears, worries and anger that may be expressed at times.

9. Understand normal reactions under the circumstances.

10. Try to exercise as much possible.

11. Sleep as time permits.

12. A tried and true rule of disaster work: when you have time eat, drink water, go to the bathroom and sleep … **Do it.**

13. Try to stay on a meal schedule.

14. Avoid trying to survive on coffee and snacks. Do not victimize yourself in this way.

15. Water is the beverage of choice.

16. Do not accede to the temptation to utilize alcohol or to otherwise self-medicate.

17. Develop the ability to make clear and calm decisions under stress. This may take some practice and be harder for some than for others.

18. Encourage your partner and other disaster suffers.

19. If you need mental health care for yourself, seek it early.

20. If your partner could use some help, give it (with their permission.)

21. Remember that assistance given on the front line often assures a quicker return to required activities.

22. If you or your Battle Buddy needs to leave the immediate area, do it.

23. Hand over other victims to interveners trained to help them.

24. Always try to make and to keep the scene secure to avoid additional injuries or other problems.

25. If your scene is not secure, tell someone who can respond to the threat.

26. Don't ignore problems that could affect your safety or the safety of those around you.

27. Make decisions to return to the scene, and / or to continue your involvement, based on your own needs and desires.

28. Encourage victims to put themselves first, before other family member or fellow sufferers.

29. Be in control of those things that are readily within your control; don't take on more than you can handle.

30. Ask questions to satisfy your concerns.

31. Remember that there may not be concrete answers readily available.

32. Ask again later.

33. Let the victims read these guidelines and suggestions as needed and as possible.

Encourage sufferers to be alert to the possible signs of alcohol and substance abuse occurring post disaster or exacerbated by the disaster itself.

The following indicators or warning signs are associated with alcohol and drug addiction, and other physical and mental disorders. Use this list in emotional first aid situations. If several symptoms are present, refer the person for alcohol and drug assessment. This list is not to be used as a substitute for a screening or qualified clinical assessment.

Physical / Emotional Indicators

- Smell of alcohol or marijuana.
- Burned fingers, burns on lips, or needle track marks on arms.
- Slurs speech or stutters, is incoherent.
- Difficulty maintaining eye contact.
- Dilated (enlarged) or constricted (pinpoint) pupils.
- Tremors (shaking or twitching of hands and eyelids).
- Hyperactive and overly energetic.
- Appears lethargic or falls asleep easily.
- Exhibits impaired coordination or unsteady gait (e.g., staggering, off balance).
- Speaks very rapidly or very slowly.
- Experiences wide mood swings (highs and lows).
- Appears fearful or anxious; experiences panic attacks.
- Appears impatient, agitated, or irritable.
- Is increasingly angry or defiant.

Personal Attitude / Behavior Indicators

- Talks about getting high, uses vocabulary typical among drug users.
- Behaves in an impulsive or inappropriate manner.
- Denies, lies, or covers up.
- Takes unnecessary risks or acts in a reckless manner.
- Breaks or bends rules, cheats.
- Misses interviews, appointments, or meetings or arrives intoxicated.
- Fails to comply with program requirements without easily verifiable reasons (may be verbally uncooperative to disguise the problem or divert attention).

Cognitive / Mental Indicators

- Has difficulty concentrating, focusing, or attending to a task
- Appears distracted or disoriented.
- Makes inappropriate or unreasonable choices.
- Has difficulty making decisions.
- Experiences short-term memory loss.
- Experiences blackout.
- Needs directions repeated frequently.
- Has difficulty recalling known details.
- Needs repeated assistance completing ordinary paperwork (e.g., application forms).

What victims might expect in personal, family, work, and financial life during and post disasters and traumatic events

Disasters and traumatic events touch all of our lives. About two-thirds of the U.S. population has reported experiencing at least one personal traumatic event before the age of 18. Many people experience trauma due to natural disasters such as floods, hurricanes, and other storms and human-caused events like mass violence and terrorism. For some survivors, disasters can remind them of earlier trauma and make it harder to recover. With good social support and coping skills, most survivors have the ability to recover and are quite resilient. For those who continue to suffer, help is available.

After a Disaster or Traumatic Event

What to Expect in a Victim's Personal Life

Anxiety, sadness and trouble sleeping are the most common responses to traumatic events. So are headaches and stomach aches, overeating and loss of appetite. Grief may be felt intensely on and off for at least a year, especially if someone has lost a loved one in the event. Anger is a common response experienced more by men, while self-blame appears more often in women. Some people will look at what their lives were like prior to a trauma and make comparisons. Others may be concerned about their own and their family's safety. Additionally, everyone has different ways of coping, which can make people act differently than they usually do.

What follows are examples of the types of emotional, behavioral, physical, and cognitive responses that are all common reactions to a disaster or other traumatic event.

What to Expect in a Victim's Family Life

The effect of a disaster or traumatic event goes far beyond its immediate devastation. It takes time for survivors to grieve and rebuild individual and family lives. Everyday routines may not return to normal for months, or even years, especially following a large-scale disaster or traumatic event. Alternate living conditions (e.g., temporary housing) can disrupt day-to-day activities and create shifts in roles and responsibilities, leading to strains in relationships. These disruptions in routine can make life unfamiliar or unpredictable and change everyone's expectations. Remember that children's stress may be a reflection of how their parents are handling the stress.

What To Expect in a Victim's Work and Financial Life

Workplace routines may change, or businesses may close altogether, if there is extensive physical damage to buildings and roads. Daily travel and commuting patterns may be disrupted because of the loss of a car or road reconstruction. The stress of a traumatic event may lead to poor work performance, and short tempers may surface at the workplace.

Those who experience work disruptions may be unable to regain their previous standard of living, and reduced income may lead to unpaid bills. Seeking financial assistance to rebuild and repair damages can add to the already high levels of stress and frustration caused by the disaster or traumatic event.

What Can Help Victims

Everyone has different ways of coping, but there are some steps to recovery from a disaster or traumatic event that are known to help many people. Start by realizing that you survived the disaster or trauma and that life doesn't have to stop.

- Talk with someone.
- Connecting with and talking to others who accept and understand your feelings is the best way to help yourself.
- Reach out to a trusted friend, family member, or faith leader and talk about how you are doing.
- Move your body. It is the next best way to relieve stress. Try deep breathing, gentle stretching, and walking. These are the simplest exercises that can help. Other types of exercise can also relieve stress (use caution when lifting heavy weights, as excess adrenaline from stress can cause muscle damage). Meditate and listen to music timed to your breathing.
- Promote physical care by eating healthy meals and snacks, getting enough rest, and drinking plenty of water. Model these behaviors for your family.
- Reestablish routines.
- Get back to doing the things you would normally do every day. This can help you regain a sense of control over your life and reduce anxiety. Know that it's okay to celebrate successes in the recovery process and have moments of joy even after a trauma. Return to doing things you enjoy as a family and spending time with friends.
- Try not to let thoughts about the disaster or trauma take over your thinking.

- If you are having difficulty making sense of the trauma or are questioning why this event happened, seek out a mental health professional or, if you prefer, speak with a trusted faith-based or spiritual leader.
- Speak with a financial advisor.
- For help with financial matters, talking with a professional financial advisor may ease your stress and the feeling that you have to manage it alone. An advisor may have useful suggestions for addressing financial concerns, and may be able to help directly or to connect you with resources to help in other ways.
- See the Advanced Directive on page 166.

Signs That Survivors Need More Help Managing Stress

Sometimes excessive ongoing stress or medical problems that existed before the disaster or trauma can make recovery difficult. Some of the more serious signs of stress include the following:

- Disorientation or confusion and difficulty communicating thoughts.
- Inability to see or hear properly.
- Limited attention span and difficulty concentrating.
- Feelings of becoming easily frustrated.
- Overwhelming guilt and self-doubt.
- Feelings of hopelessness.
- Frequent mood swings or continuous crying.
- Colds or flu-like symptoms.
- Reluctance to leave home.
- Fear of crowds, strangers, or being alone.
- Increased use of illegal drugs, alcohol, or prescription medication.
- Worsening of existing medical problems.

If your clients or a member of their family experience trouble coping, or these signs continue for more than 2 to 4 weeks, ask for help. Refer them to a counselor or mental health professional, or see the Helpful Resources on the following page. In the workplace, you may be able to get assistance from your human resources department or your company's Employee Assistance Program.

Other Resources

Information Clearinghouses

National Mental Health Information Center (NMHIC)
P.O. Box 42557, Washington, DC 20015

(800) 789-2647 (English and Español)
(866) 889-2647 (TDD)
www.mentalhealth.samhsa.gov

National Clearinghouse for Alcohol and Drug Information (NCADI)
P.O. Box 2345,
Rockville, MD 20847-2345

(800) 729-6686 (English and Español)
(800) 487-4889 (TDD)
www.ncadi.samhsa.gov

Treatment Locators

Mental Health Services Locator
(800) 789-2647 (English and Español)
(866) 889-2647 (TDD)
www.mentalhealth.samhsa.gov/databases

Substance Abuse Treatment Facility Locator

(800) 662-HELP (4357) (Toll-Free, 24-Hour
English and Español Treatment Referral Service)

(800) 487-4889 (TDD)
www.findtreatment.samhsa.gov

Hotlines

National Suicide Prevention Lifeline
(800) 273-TALK (8255)

SAMHSA National Helpline
(800) 662-HELP (4357) (English and Español)
(800) 487-4889 (TDD)

Workplace Helpline

(800) WORKPLACE (967-5752)
www.workplace.samhsa.gov/helpline/helpline.htm

U.S. Department of Health and Human Services

Substance Abuse and Mental Health Services Administration
      Center for Mental Health Services
www.samhsa.gov

A Final Note

Find those indicators of resiliency present in individual victims. Encourage them to play to their strengths. Help victims follow the guidelines presented above and others as may become necessary, depending on the specific situation. Do not make the assumption that victims of disaster are without personal emotional resources. Encourage each to rely on themselves and to do what they can. Be there for support, referral or evacuation. Expect that victims will wish to work within the disaster area and generally should not be dissuaded from doing so. If they are in danger, remove them from the threat or remove the threat. Do not expose yourself to additional threat or harm. Your ability to assist will be compromised if you do. Always listen carefully to the victim. Observe carefully what is going on. Consider what is being told to you and ask good and pointed questions as needed. This will not be a time for euphemisms. Treat the victim/sufferer as you think you would like to be treated if your roles were reversed.

Chapter 6

Altered Standards of Care: A subject no one wants to talk about

**Remember and never forget:
Prepare yourself for this eventuality or don't get involved.**

A highly competent medical disaster worker related a relevant and illustrative story. This provider usually works with acute trauma victims and within a well-equipped medical center. Following his return to work from a devastating disaster, he did not know how he could live with himself. During the disaster because of limited resources, all he could do for a medical patient was to hold her hand while she died. In his medical center, he could have probably saved her life. On site hand-holding was the best care available. Adjusting to these realities took some time. He was not prepared for such an eventuality and felt guilty that the generally acceptable standard of care to which he was trained could not be met.

This topic is the subject of much controversy and debate in professional circles. Traditionally, health care responders are trained and held to the standard of care of their profession when rendering aid. Nothing less is acceptable. The public understands and even demands this level of care. For example, citizens in this country expect that if they are injured or sick and call for help, that help will be there for them. One reason that so many people do not prepare adequately for a disaster is that they believe that emergency care would be available just as it is during normal, non-disaster times. This is not the case.

In a study reported by Medscape (Reese, 2010), 10,000 physicians from all specialty areas were surveyed. Among other issues regarding ethics, two questions addressed care given patients at the end of their life. In response to the question, "Would you ever recommend or give life-sustaining therapy when you judged that it was futile?" about 5300 of the physicians answered. 23.6% answered that they would continue care they knew to be futile. Another 37% said that they would not. Most of the responding physicians, about 39.4%, said that any such decision that they might make would depend on the circumstances. Most would probably agree that such responses from physicians are not unusual given how they are trained. For responders and interveners questions such as what constitutes futile, is there moral justification for continuing or ending care, and what is the burden involved to the patient and family, must be considered and understood.

Additionally, what does a health care provider do when family members say that they want everything done? What does that mean, how should it be considered, and under what circumstances? Patient's wishes and advanced directives must be taken into account in an ethical and meaningful fashion. Some believe that the family should be the final arbiter in end-of-life situations. The fear of litigation and of violating an individual's or a family's desires was also discussed. In a comment on the survey results by Dr. Nancy Berlinger, an ethicist with the Hastings Center in Garrison, New York, she presses the point. "Caring for the patient always comes first. Duty of care is to the patient." Issues of palliative care were also raised and distinguished from medical care. As the survey was analyzed, the viewpoints of the respondents became more complex and conditional. What might have been discerned as a level of consensus in the area, has actually made this area of concern more difficult; more difficult at a time when such consensus may be very important. Greater solidarity among respondents was seen to some degree with the second related survey question, "Would you ever consider halting life-sustaining therapy because the family demanded it, even if you believed that it was premature?" A majority of the respondents said that they would not discontinue care (54.5%). 16.3% said that they would discontinue care under the stated circumstances. The other 29.2% said that it would depend on the situation. Some said that they would hold a meeting with all concerned. Others would also include an investigation into the motives of those recommending discontinuation. Decisions will be complex and the consequences of such decisions made under disaster or crisis situations will probably continue to be judged under non-disaster or non-crisis situations. This increases the conundrum and seems to provide less clarity than is needed.

Disasters pose a counter-testimony to the training that most receive. With overwhelming numbers of victims, and supplies that can never be adequate under such circumstances, the care mandated must be first aimed at those who can benefit the most from it. Additionally, it must reach the greatest number possible of such victims. All possible care cannot be rendered for all victims of a disaster. And, certainly it cannot be rendered to those who will not survive even with such care. These are less-than-ideal circumstances and we must be prepared to provide less-than-ideal care when it is called for. In so doing, survival potential may be enhanced for those with the greatest opportunity to survive. This is not advocacy for not giving the best care possible to all affected. It is meant to suggest that we must respond realistically to the circumstances under which we may find ourselves working. How will we know? The circumstances will dictate the answer. It is important that we understand what is happening around us.

The usual standard of care may not be possible to achieve under a disaster scenario.

Understand the application of sufficient care. Expect that the standard may shift from standard of care to sufficiency of care. Adjust your mindset to this eventuality.

- Recognize that people will die.

- Recognize it again; this time at the level of your gut or feelings.

- Sufficiency of care may need to be the standard of care in a disaster.

- Expect sufficiency of care to be the standard of care under most disaster situations. If the circumstances are better, great. Just do not expect them to be.

- Plan for this lack of standard of care mentally and emotionally.

- Discuss the concept with other responders pre-incident.

- Discuss this concept with other interveners during the incident itself.

Provide standard of care, when possible. Return to the standard of care at the earliest possible time. Altered standards should be discontinued as soon as it is possible to return to the usual standards of care. We should go out of the business of altered standards of care as soon as possible. Our goal is always to provide care at the highest level possible and to never provide less than this even though conditions and resources may so dictate.

Work this out for yourself before being deployed. The head work is important for all emotional first aiders to do. Without it, we are not ready for what will come.

Allow for your feelings about this and your resistance to it. None of us are currently trained this way.

Discourage self-blame by others. Resist blaming yourself. Seek professional help early to resolve difficult issues, as you need such help. Talk to a confidant, a close family member … someone who will not make light of your concerns and feelings. Such a person will not attempt to fix you, to change your feelings or solve your dilemma. Professional help is important too. Try to find a behavioral health professional that has experience in crisis and disaster situations. If you are a member of a response team, you may have a mental health specialist on your team. Seek out this person and let them assist you in the areas of your concern: stress and overall response to the work you do or to the situations in which you have found yourself.

Remember that in a disaster, needs will outweigh resources. That condition defines a disaster. All crises to which you may respond may not occur during a disaster. Disaster Crisis Intervention involves added concerns for which you must be prepared. Know what you are best prepared to do. If you function well within a disaster, know this. If you deal with individual or group crises on a day-to-day basis and can do this well but may not be able to handle the additional stress, requirements and conditions brought on by a disaster, know this also and respond accordingly. Sense where your personal energy is directing you. Don't fight this energy. Go with it. You will be on target most of the time.

Remind yourself that all of your available resources must provide the greatest good for the greatest number of people. Also, remind yourself that all resources must be allocated to those having the best chance of benefiting from them. In our best professional judgment, we will often have to make these decisions.

- How to manage and comfort those who will die. Remember that helping the dying to end their life with dignity is an important aspect of our care for them.

- Help the greatest number by providing what you have to offer.

- Resist the guilt that results from not accepting this.

- Prepare yourself to surrender the usual standard of care when necessary and to provide care that is at least sufficient under the existing circumstances.

Allow this to be okay in disaster situations. Recognize that it is okay because you are prevented from giving a higher level of care due to the totality of the circumstances, not due to your own lack of knowledge and skill.

Additionally, be prepared for your judgments under crisis and disaster conditions to be judged by others under non-crisis and disaster conditions. This can be a scary proposition. This may also be the reason that not all professionals and paraprofessionals will respond to crisis situations. It may also be why not just anyone can do this type of response. In many ways it is analogous to the difference between working in an office and working in an emergency room. Not all can do both. Some who work well in an emergency room may not be able to adjust to a disaster or altered standards of care environment. Refer to the legal chapter in this book. Also, do those things during your interventions that will document and explain what you did and why you did it, and the circumstances surrounding your decisions. Document everything. It will serve you well later on.

Final Note

Many times, political, religious, cultural, legal and policy considerations conflict with actions and outcomes or personal opinions of how things should be. For example, in a disaster scenario, FEMA has laws and rules to follow that prohibit them from doing or being involved in certain things. Similarly, doctors and other healthcare professionals have ethical limits. Authority, such as jurisdiction, home rule, county judges and the like, have the authority, not the intervener or other professional. Views of practices and outcomes are not the final word. Educating yourself about the law and policies in force is a requirement of a professional. In the alternative to accepting what is, you can always work to change the law or policy. (W. Campbell, personal communication, January 17, 2013).

Chapter 7

Hostile Environments:
Knowing what to get into–
Knowing what to stay out of

Remember and never forget: Prepare for the worst.

It is likely that if you respond to a disaster, you will find one uncertainty followed by another.

A long-standing standard among crisis interveners is that knowing what to stay out of is just as important as knowing where to become involved. The rule may be more important than thought at first glance. Once you have decided to become involved in a crisis intervention or disaster response, you are committed. There may be legal standards and duties that you will read about in Chapter 10. Regardless of the law, once you are involved in a high stress situation for which you are unprepared, the likelihood of you experiencing personal crisis increases. If you experience crisis in your own life, you will be of no value to the crisis or disaster victims who are looking to you for help. Additionally, because you are in crisis, other interveners will have to attend to you since you have now become another victim. In so doing, you and they have reduced the resources available to the primary victims of the crisis situation. What is wrong with that picture? Note that nothing written here diminishes the importance of force protection.* This is a vital component of any response capability. However, adding to the problems already encountered by lack of preparation or by failure to recognize the personal pitfalls of being a responder is less than helpful, to say the very least. Note also that in disaster or emergency response, the

---

* *Force protection: preventive measures taken to mitigate hostile actions against responders, family members, resources, facilities, and critical information.*

assignment of team responsibilities may designate that force protection is the primary role of the responder / intervener.

Sometimes our training conveys the unintended message that, because of our training, we can handle anything that comes our way; we are not susceptible to the crisis experience as are others. This is a stretch at best and actually very far from the truth in this matter. Not everyone can handle everything. There is no disgrace in that, nor does that degrade us as professionals. Knowing one's strengths and weaknesses, and acting according to what you know, is a professionally enhancing act. Knowing what you can do, and what may be best for you not to do, may well save your life and the life of those requiring Crisis Interventions, both physically and emotionally. Think about it and heed the warning. Discretion is always the better part of valor in these incidents. The effectiveness of your assistance to sufferers may depend on your ability to make these distinctions. If your gut says no, don't go.

A priori understanding of a disaster or crisis scene is not an easy task. Being there and being part of the environment and all of its uncertainties is a lesson in itself. It needs to be learned quickly if you are to survive and be effective in performing your job. Take the time to talk to others who have successfully completed a Crisis Intervention or a disaster deployment. Realizing that second-hand accounts may not be totally accurate, they may still give you some insight into your future deployments. Ask cogent questions designed to get the real information. Observe and listen carefully to the accounts that are presented. Think about what you have heard and ask clarifying questions as you may need to get as close as you can to situational accuracy. Notice what is said and what is not. Pay attention to news reports of difficult situations that may form the basis of your involvement. Imagine your involvement and ask yourself if you are really prepared to serve. Doing this ahead of time benefits not only you, but also your team members and the victims you will undoubtedly encounter. If being part of a crisis response is too much for you as determined by your honest reflection, reconsider how you might best be involved. Get more training. Defer from deployments about which you have major personal concerns. Redirect your energies as needed. Everyone cannot do everything. Certainly there is no shame or disgrace in recognizing that. In fact, you may be doing many a great service. If direct encounters are difficult, perhaps you can work indirectly on a crisis situation or disaster event. Support is as important as direct services. The important thing is that you not be surprised by getting involved in situations that are really too much for you, both physically and mentally. Also, it will serve you and others well if you come to these conclusions before an actual event. The other side of the same coin is that you may be better able to handle the gross uncertainties of an intervention more effectively than you ever imagined. If you have trained well, rehearsed your skills, been realistic about your own strengths, and have adjusted your mindset accordingly, you may be able to be in the right place at the right time. Know yourself and then do your job. Either way, you will do the right thing.

It must be noted that hostile environments are not limited to the physical terrain, surrounding threats, needy victims, and compromised resources. Lack of support, hidden personal agendas, political and bureaucratic agendas can create a toxic environment that is equally dangerous.

The importance of support systems during disaster operations cannot be over emphasized. Personal relationships may provide support at first but at the end of the day, the remaining team member may lack the needed support. Given the reality of personnel rotation, some care must be taken by the team member to establish new and/or to maintain ongoing support relationships on the scene; as well as to keep in touch with those back home. This can be accomplished via mail and phone calls.

It may be assumed by the casual observer, or the new worker, that those who have been there for some time have the necessary support in place. This may not be true in actuality.

Briefings should cover this area carefully. All team members should take personal responsibility for developing and maintaining new and ongoing liaisons for their own personal survival.

The following example might help illustrate the institutional problems mentioned above. Political and bureaucratic agendas often complicate the providing of services to those who need them. In this actual example, disguised for obvious reasons, the attitude of leadership often was that, "If I didn't think of it, it isn't going to happen." The attitude was critical and seldom helpful. It was not critical in the sense of constructiveness but of obstructiveness. In one specific instance, a proposal to develop a referral base for those working in the field that needed it when none existed locally was rejected on political and interpersonal grounds. It was hard to tell whether this was the result of turf battles that go on all around, or governmental and bureaucratic inaction or inability. One thing was certain: those who were frustrated by the lack of services remained frustrated. The result was that those who needed the benefit of the services were not going to get them.

Administrative procedures were in place, but ill-defined. The "loop" was unclear. The intervener in this example was told that following a certain procedure was necessary for such a proposal to be made. In actuality, the disaster worker went to unusual ends to ascertain the correct system to use. Although the procedure indicated was followed, certain actors who should have been in the loop were not included. Perhaps others should have been included or excluded as well. Systems were established to block progress, not to assist it. This resulted in much frustration among staff members and other workers. There was no counter-proposal offered by management. The project was left to wither for lack of nourishment.

Interestingly enough, the intervener felt little of the stress experienced by others. Perhaps this was true because she would be leaving soon from the area of operations. Factor in that her investment was a strictly professional one. She believed that is why some of this ineffectiveness affected her very little one way or the other; or so she said.

This was a major operation headed by a major disaster response and relief organization. It was apparent that this organization had some severe problems working with ideas and personnel. Because they are broad-based, she saw these same problems on a local basis back home. Maybe all of this was related. This organization had troubles working and playing well with others, to quote an old report card category.

In attempting to develop services for those in the affected community, the intervener was contacted by the agency director and blamed for creating a problem by getting involved with the community she was there to assist. She believed that she did her best to explain to the director about the procedures followed and the need that existed. Once this issue was reduced, the director continued to belittle and nitpick the specific way in which she followed the established procedures. There seemed to be no way to get around this impasse; one that should never have occurred in the first place.

Hostility within a disaster environment can come from many sources. Some are readily expected; some are not. The result of this tiny tale is that nothing was resolved and nothing was done to assist this area of the community. The effort was stopped in its tracks. Soon the intervener left the area of operations to resume her usual life. Subsequently her performance evaluation reflected what she had experienced. Why would she want to ever do this again?

Lessons learned take many forms. We may not be able to expect that we can manage every crisis; but we must be prepared to manage each crisis. Additionally, we must be unconditionally constructive and always prepared to do what is necessary when and if it is necessary.

A Final Note

Prepare well. Stay safe. Understand the disaster environment. Expect the politics. Be unconditionally constructive in all you do.

FIGURE 7.1 EMERGENCY SUPPORT FUNCTIONS

Emergency Support Functions

Emergency Support Functions (ESFs) is the grouping of governmental and certain private sector capabilities into an organizational structure to provide support, resources, program implementation, and services that are most likely needed to save lives, protect property and the environment, restore essential services and critical infrastructure, and help victims and communities return to normal following domestic incidents.

Emergency Support Functions

- ESF1   Transportation
- ESF2   Communications
- ESF3   Public Works and Engineering
- ESF4   Firefighting
- ESF5   Emergency Management
- ESF6   Mass Care, Housing, and Human Services
- ESF7   Resources Support
- ESF8   Public Health and Medical Services
- ESF9   Urban Search and Rescue
- ESF10 Oil and Hazardous Materials Response
- ESF11 Agriculture and Natural Resources
- ESF12 Energy
- ESF13 Public Safety and Security
- ESF14 Long-term Community Recovery and Mitigation
- ESF15 External Affairs

(Continued on the next page)

Emergency Support Functions *(Continued)*

There are 15 ESFs, and Health and Human Services (HHS) is the primary agency responsible for Emergency Support Functions (ESF) 8 – Public Health and Medical Services. ESF 8 is coordinated by the Secretary of HHS principally through the Assistant Secretary for Preparedness and Response (ASPR). ESF 8 resources can be activated through the Stafford Act or the Public Health Service Act.

ESF 8 – Public Health and Medical Services

ESF 8 – Public Health and Medical Services provides the mechanism for coordinated Federal assistance to supplement State, Tribal, and local resources in response to the following:

- Public health and medical care needs
- Veterinary and/or animal health issues in coordination with the U.S. Department of Agriculture (USDA)
- Potential or actual incidents of national significance
- A developing potential health and medical situation

ESF 8 involves supplemental assistance to state, tribal, and jurisdictional governments in identifying and meeting the public health and medical needs of victims of major disasters or public health and medical emergencies. This support is categorized in the following functional areas:

- Assessment of public health/medical needs
- Public health surveillance
- Medical care personnel
- Medical equipment and supplies
- Patient movement
- Hospital care
- Outpatient services
- Victim decontamination
- Safety and security of human drugs, biologics, medical devices, veterinary drugs, etc.
- Blood products and services
- Food safety and security
- Agriculture feed safety and security

Emergency Support Functions *(Continued)*

- Worker health and safety
- All hazard consultation and technical assistance and support
- Mental health and substance abuse care
- Public health and medical information
- Vector control
- Potable water/wastewater and solid waste disposal, and other environmental health issues
- Victim identification/mortuary services
- Veterinary services.
- Federal public health and medical assistance consists of medical materiel, personnel, and technical assistance.

Health and Medical Response Lead Partners

HHS leads and coordinates the overall health and medical response to national-level incidents through coordination, along with the following:

- Department of Agriculture
- Department of Transportation
- Department of Defense
- Department of Veterans Affairs
- Department of State
- Agency for International Development
- Department of Energy
- Environmental Protection Agency
- Department of Homeland Security
- General Services Administration
- Department of Interior
- U.S. Postal Service
- Department of Justice
- American Red Cross
- Department of Labor

Assistant Secretary for Preparedness and Response (ASPR), 200 Independence Ave., SW, Washington, DC 20201.

U.S. Department of Health and Human Services

(Continued on the next page)

FIGURE 7.2 – THE NATIONAL DISASTER RECOVERY SUPPORT FUNCTIONS

The National Disaster Recovery Framework introduces six new Recovery Support Functions that are led by designated federal coordinating agencies at the national level.

Recovery Support Functions involve partners in the local, state and tribal governments and private and nonprofit sectors not typically involved in emergency support functions but critically needed in disaster recovery. These new partners may include public and private organizations that have experience with permanent housing financing, economic development, advocacy for underserved populations and long-term community planning. The processes used for facilitating recovery are more flexible, context based and collaborative in approach than the task-oriented approach used during the response phase of an incident.

Recovery processes should be scalable and based on demonstrated recovery needs. Each Recovery Support Function has a designated coordinating agency along with primary agencies and supporting organizations with programs relevant to the functional area. The Recovery Support Function Coordinating Agency, with the assistance of the Federal Emergency Management Agency, provides leadership, coordination and oversight for that particular agency. When coordinating agencies are activated to lead a Recovery Support Function, primary agencies and supporting organizations are expected to be responsive to the function related communication and coordination needs.

Health and Social Services

Coordinating Agency:
>   Department of Health and Human Services

Primary Agencies:
>   Corporation for National and Community Service, Department of Homeland Security *(Federal Emergency Management Agency/National Preparedness and Protection Directive and Civil Rights and Civil Liberties)*
>
>   Department of Interior
>
>   Department of Justice
>
>   Department of Labor
>
>   Education Department and Veterans Affairs

Health and Social Services *(Continued)*

Supporting Organizations:

> Department of Transportation
>
> Small Business Administration
>
> Department of Treasury
>
> Department of Agriculture
>
> Veterans Affairs
>
> American Red Cross
>
> National Organizations Active in Disasters

Mission

The Health and Social Services Recovery Support Function mission is for the Federal Government to assist locally-led recovery efforts in the restoration of the public health, health care and social services networks to promote the resilience, health and well-being of affected individuals and communities.

FIGURE 7.3 – NATIONAL DISASTER RECOVERY FRAMEWORK

National Disaster Recovery Framework

Function

The core recovery capability for health and social services is the ability to restore and improve health and social services networks to promote the resilience, health, independence and well being of the whole community. The Health and Social Services RSF outlines the Federal framework to support locally-led recovery efforts to address public health, health care facilities and coalitions, and essential social services needs. For the purposes of this RSF, the use of the term health will refer to and include public health, behavioral health and medical services.

This Annex establishes (1) a Federal focal point for coordinating Federal recovery efforts specifically for health and social services needs; and, (2) a Federal operational framework outlining how Federal agencies plan to support local health and social services recovery efforts. This framework is flexible and can adjust during a disaster to complement local efforts, as needed.

(Continued on the next page)

Pre-Disaster: The Health and Social Services Recovery Support Function *(Continued)*

- Incorporates planning for the transition from response to recovery into preparedness and operational plans, in close collaboration with ESFs #3, #6, #8 and #11.

- Incorporates planning for the transition from post-incident recovery operations back to a steady-state into preparedness and operational plans.

- Develops strategies to address recovery issues for health, behavioral health and social services – particularly the needs of response and recovery workers, children, seniors, people living with disabilities, people with functional needs, people from diverse cultural origins, people with limited English proficiency and underserved populations.

- Promotes the principles of sustainability, resilience and mitigation into preparedness and operational plans.

Post-Disaster: The Health and Social Services Recovery Support Function

- Maintains situational awareness to identify and mitigate potential recovery obstacles during the response phase.

- Leverages response, emergency protection measures and hazard mitigation resources during the response phase to expedite recovery.

- Provides technical assistance in the form of impact analyses and supports recovery planning of public health, health care and human services infrastructure.

- Conducts Federal Health and Social Services Recovery Support Function assessments with primary agencies.

- Identifies and coordinates Federal Health and Social Services specific missions with primary agencies

- When activated by the Federal Disaster Recovery Coordinator, the primary and supporting departments and agencies deploy in support of the Health and Social Services Recovery Support Function mission, as appropriate.

- Establishes communication and information-sharing forum(s) for Health and Social Services RSF stakeholders with the State and/or community.

- Coordinates and leverages applicable Federal resources for health and social services.

- Develops and implements a plan to transition from Federal Health and Social Services recovery operations back to a steady-state.
- Identifies and coordinates with other local, State, Tribal and Federal partners to assess food, animal, water and air conditions to ensure safety.
- Evaluates the effectiveness of Federal Health and Social Services recovery efforts.
- Provides technical assistance in the form of impact analyses and recovery planning support of public health, health care, and human services infrastructure.
- Identifies and coordinates with other local, State, Tribal and Federal partners the assessment of food, animal, water and air conditions to ensure their safety.

Outcomes for the Health and Social Services Recovery Support Function

- Restore the capacity and resilience of essential health and social services to meet ongoing and emerging post-disaster community needs.
- Encourage behavioral health systems to meet the behavioral health needs of affected individuals, response and recovery workers, and the community.
- Promote self-sufficiency and continuity of the health and well-being of affected individuals; particularly the needs of children, seniors, people living with disabilities whose members may have additional functional needs, people from diverse origins, people with limited English proficiency, and underserved populations.
- Assist in the continuity of essential health and social services, including schools.
- Reconnect displaced populations with essential health and social services.
- Protect the health of the population and response and recovery workers from the longer-term effects of a post-disaster environment.
- Promote clear communications and public health messaging to provide accurate, appropriate and accessible information; ensure information is developed and disseminated in multiple mediums, multi-lingual formats, alternative formats, is age-appropriate and user-friendly and is accessible to underserved populations.

September 2011

Chapter 8

Preparation: "The Orange Bag Denial"

Remember and never forget: Get your stuff together now.

If denial exists anywhere, it exists here. The seemingly unconscious process of refusing those implements of survival that might be needed during a disaster scenario because acceptance also means acceptance of the likelihood of a disaster occurring, is the focus here. Disasters do and will occur. As Sherif and Sherif stated in their seminal work, *An Outline of Social Psychology*, 1956, refusal of the implements of survival denies that reality. Acceptance confirms it. Perhaps acknowledgement of this process will impact the individual's frame of reference or psychological structuring, and thereby affect observed behavior

The Issue

Perhaps the reason that people refuse to prepare for the onset of a disaster relates to the new psychological term: "Orange Bag Denial." (Greenstone, 2009). Manmade and natural disasters will occur. One has only to look around themselves to confirm this reality.

Many will remember a few years ago when, in a prominent way, a product came on the market that promised to provide sufficient supplies to help an individual to survive the first 72 hours of a disaster, man-made or natural. These provisions were carefully provided in an orange canvas backpack that sold for about $30 - $35. The supplies provided would have probably cost more than the $35 price tag if one were to purchase them separately. In addition to the flashlight, batteries, water, food, tools, and the like, the size of the backpack allowed for personal gear such as extra clothing and other supplies. Altogether the pack was still light enough for even the slightest individual to carry the bag and to move around with ease.

The Search

Being a preparer, my personal "go bag" has been ready for the various circumstances in which one might find himself. Even so, this new orange bag was of some interest. As one might expect, it was quickly determined that they were readily available at most super stores in the area. What was found there was surprising and yet not completely unexpected.

An individual search of the store began. (This was probably because of an aversion to asking for directions.) Anyway, the bags were nowhere to be found even though advertised. Finally, several employees were approached for directions to the bags. They were found standing together obviously discussing profit and loss statements. They were not knowledgeable about the bags and could not recall seeing them on the store shelves. The manager was summoned. He knew about the bags. He explained that they had been removed from the shelves because they were not selling; an inkling that something was afoot. The manager explained that he was about to return the bags to the supplier but that they were still in the store stock room.

In the stock room, a bin was full of the orange emergency bags. The manager was asked if the bags were still available for sale. He said that they were and that he would sell them at an incredibly good price for as many of them as were desired. The price was so good, all were purchased. An immediate thought was that they could be given as Christmas or Chanukah gifts. Who knew?

After the bags were purchased and loaded into the car, they were transported to be used as presents.

The Results

When it was mentioned to a very smart wife that the bags would be given as gifts, she warned against such actions. Not fully understanding the issues, this author argued, disagreed and finally acquiesced. This proved to be the correct choice. The rest was amazing.

There were several family members and fellow preparers, to whom this writer was close personally, and to whom the bags might be given. Not so much as a holiday gift, but later because of concern about their readiness if something bad happened.

Most of the few close friends to whom the orange gifts were given were visibly and verbally shocked by this expression of kindness. To a person, their eyes bugged, they appeared stunned. They asked why such a gift would be given to them. Several were shocked and asked, "Do you know something that I don't?"

Therein was born the concept of the Orange Bag Denial. Acceptance of the gift would also mean an acceptance of the possibility that a disaster might occur and that the contents of the orange bag might have to be utilized. The alternative, not to accept the bag, as a few did, in essence was avoidance and a denial of such a possibility. In other words, "If I do not take the bag designed for a disaster, maybe I will be spared the disaster. On the other hand, if I accept the bag, then also I have to accept the fact that a disaster may occur for which I may need these supplies."

Some of the Related Numbers and Findings

There are at least four stages of preparedness denial. According to Eric Holdeman (2008), Director of Emergency Management for King County, Texas, the four stages are:

1. It won't happen,
2. If it does happen, it won't happen to me,
3. If it does happen to me, it won't be that bad; and
4. If it happens and it is bad, there is nothing that I can do to stop it anyway.

In an August 2006 poll conducted by Time Magazine, it was reported that most American citizens were not prepared for a disaster and had their heads in the sand. Half surveyed said they had experienced a disaster. Only 16% of those said that they were adequately prepared for another disaster. Many justified their poor preparation by indicating that they did not need to prepare because that they did not live in areas of high risk for any kind of disaster (Ripley, 2006).

Facts seem to support the assertion that 91% of Americans live in places of significant risk to some type of disaster situation that could dramatically affect their life. This study was conducted by the Hazards and Vulnerability Research Institute at the University of South Carolina (Ripley, 2006). There seems to be a fine line, according to this quoted article, between optimism and foolishness. In a country whose citizens, many times, distrust its leaders, the vast majority continue to think that in a disaster our government, local, state, and national, will quickly come to our aid as in non-disaster times. The response to Hurricane Katrina is the strongest current counter-testimony to this ill-conceived belief.

A Final Note

Maybe all of this preparation is just the hyperactivity of a psychologically-oriented mind. (Greenstone & Leviton, 2011). Who knows? I've got my bag! Or, maybe we need to get our heads out of the sand, and readjust to the real world for which we need to prepare.

FIGURE 8.1 – FIELD PERSONAL EQUIPMENT CHECK LIST
THE 2-3-4 RULE (2010)

The 2-3-4 Rule

2 bags
> One personal small bag to be carried (Ready Bag)
> One large bag to be shipped or palletized (Main Flight Bag)

3 days of food, one MRE meal

4 quarts of water with one quart in Ready Bag

FIGURE 8.2 – WHAT TO BRING

What to Bring

The following list is to use when preparing for deployment. This list is devised so that all deployed team members are self-sufficient and able to care for themselves.

- Two bags are to be utilized. First, a large MAIN BAG for shipping or for palletization which will probably not be available in transit or for up to several days. This bag needs to be rugged and smart in design with a capacity of 4500 cubic inches or better.

- The second bag is a smaller READY BAG to carry items needed in flight. The Ready Bag is your carry-on with personal items. Remember your Ready Bag must meet commercial air carriers requirements for overhead bins if flying. Most folks use a backpack.

- Make sure your name is on both bags.

- The Main Flight bags must weigh less than 50 pounds if flying commercial.

FIGURE 8.3 – MAIN FLIGHT BAG

Use the following list as a guide. It will take a deployment or two before you know what to carry.

MAIN FLIGHT BAG "72 hour Pack"

CLOTHING

Long durable trousers . . . . 1–6 pair
Long sleeve durable shirt . . . . 1–2 each
Durable shorts . . . . 1–2 pair
Distinguishing "T" shirts . . . . 2–4 each
Distinguishing polo shirts . . . . 1–6 each
Boots . . . . 1 pair
Tennis shoes . . . . 1 pair
Shower shoes . . . . 1 pair
Bandana . . . . 1–2 each
Underwear . . . . 3–6 plus
Socks . . . . 3–6 plus
Swimwear 1
Camp clothes . . . . as needed

COLD WEATHER – ADDITIONAL CLOTHING

Long johns – polypro's . . . . 2–3 each
Wool sweater . . . . 1 each
Down jackets/Coats . . . . 1 each
   (polar guard)
Gloves or mittens . . . . 1–2 pair
Wool socks . . . . 1–2 pair
Cold weather boots . . . . 1 pair

COOKING AND FOOD

Knife, spoon and fork set
36 hours of rations/MREs
Cup
High energy snacks

SLEEPING

Sleeping bag (+15 degrees or more, depending on climate)

Foam pad

Ground cloth

Pillow – inflatable

MISCELLANEOUS

Head lamp (2nd light source)

Extra batteries/bulbs

Matches in waterproof container

Face mask/Dust mask

Goggles/Safety glasses

Tape, safety pens, sewing kit

Towels, wash cloth

Hand mirror

550/P cord 50'

Large trash bags

Nail clippers, etc.

FIGURE 8.4 – READY BAG "24-HOUR PACK"

READY BAG "24-hour Pack"

Must have with you:

Organizational ID and driver's license

Money and credit cards

Passport or birth certificate (out of country)

Emergency phone numbers

CLOTHING

Hat – Ball cap/Boonie . . . . 1 each

Rain Gear . . . . 1 set

Bandana . . . . 1 each

BDU* – Consider carrying one pair of BDU pants and T-shirt in a zip lock bag. Socks and underwear in zip lock bag.

Battle Dress Uniform – many pockets, just the right size in just the right place.

PERSONAL PROTECTION

Eye protection . . . . 1 set

Ear plugs . . . . 1–2 sets

Leather work gloves . . . . 1–2 sets

Flash light/s with spare batteries. . . . . 1–2 each

Personal first aid kit . . . . 1 each

PERSONAL GEAR

Razor/blades	Shaving Cream
Toothbrush/paste	Sunscreen
Comb/brush	Deodorant
Shampoo	Bar soap
Hand lotion	Hand wipes
Facial tissue	Toilet tissue
Eye wash (Visine)	Lip balm
Insect repellant	Dog tags
Medication (14 day supply)	Glasses and sun glasses
Foot Care (moleskin, powder)	Detergent (clothing)

MEDICAL EQUIPMENT
(as required and authorized by your training and specialty)

Stethoscope. . . . . 1 each

Trauma shears . . . . 1 pair

Bandage shears . . . . 1 pair

Pen light. . . . . 1 each

Pens . . . . 5–6 each

Note pads. . . . . 1–2 each

Latex gloves. . . . . Several

PERSONAL FIRST–AID KIT
Every member should carry a personal first–aid kit in the left cargo pocket of their BDUs. Your items will fit nicely in a small zip lock bag and should include:

Band–Aids . . . . 12 each

2" x 2" or 3" x 3" gauze . . . . 6 each

Betadine pads . . . . 6 each

Moleskin . . . . 1 each

Small roll of gauze . . . . 1 each

Triangular bandage. . . . . 1–2 each

Antibiotic ointment . . . . 4 each

FIGURE 8.5 – PROHIBITED ITEMS

PROHIBITED ITEMS

Do not carry the following: *(Please check with TSA before flying)*

Explosives	Compressed gas
Radioactive material	Guns
Ammunition	Corrosives
Poison	Infectious substance
Magnetized material	Oxidizers
Flammable liquid or solid	Knives
Aerial flares	Smoke signals
Mace	Pepper spray
Propane/Stove fuel	Aerosols
CO2 cartridges	Thermometers (mercury)
Lighter fluid	Wet batteries
Smoke detectors	Expensive jewelry
Perishable foods	Curling irons/Hot rollers
Alcoholic Beverages	Drugs (illegal)

Chapter 9

Response Protocols: Waiting for the Word

Remember and never forget: If you are not called, do not go.

Stand in the door. Lean forward. But don't jump in if you are not called. A glance at the personal reports and newspaper accounts of what happens when a disaster or major crisis situation occurs should tell this story to almost anyone. If an emergency happens in the street in front of your house, that may be different. If the disaster happens some distance away, wait to be called before responding. Get ready to go, but don't do it. Let those in charge know that you are available, but don't just show up. The problems get worse from there. A disaster is an occurrence of almost any size when the needs of the situation and its victims are greater than the resources available to respond to those needs. Unexpected, unrequested, and unaccounted for responders may add to the enormity of the already occurring disaster.

If you are serious about emergency and disaster response, join a team that does these things and trains its members to do it well. Federal teams are always looking for qualified professionals in many different fields. State and local teams are preparing also and could probably use the help. Some pay and some do not. Medical Reserve Corps have become quite active across this nation as are the American Red Cross and Salvation Army.

As was said earlier, the rule of thumb for most teams and organizations that respond to crisis and disaster situations is that if you are not called, **don't just show up.** Do the training. Assemble your response gear. Be ready, willing, able and well-prepared to go when called. Let your team know of your availability and how quickly you can be on the move to the designated location or staging area. **Don't just show up.**

The reasons for this cautionary tone will seem obvious to most, but not all reading it. Almost everyone wants to help when they hear that an emergency has occurred. This desire to help is good on the one hand and can be counterproductive on the other hand. Getting on a plane or in a car with your friends and colleagues and "going to help for a few days" may cause great confusion at the site or staging area and prevent trained and coordinated teams from reaching their destination in a timely fashion. Clogging the airways or the highways serves no one and could endanger those who are waiting for the help to arrive. Do-gooders have no place at a disaster scene. Trained and coordinated emergency personnel do. If you must go regardless of the consequences, at least coordinate with those who are in charge of the response and be sure that they can use your services. Take with you, in addition to your professional supplies, enough food, water, shelter, waste disposal gear, sleeping gear, and other survival supplies so that your arrival will not put added burden on those who already have limited means. Expect nothing from your host if you arrive when you are not called, requested, or needed. Assume that they have nothing to spare and that you will probably be operating on your own. If the conditions are not as stark, so much the better for you.

Disaster, emergency, and crisis response, regardless of the situation, needs to be carefully coordinated and regulated to achieve the best and most helpful results. The size of the event is not as important as the coordination of those services and service providers that are needed. The emergency, and the often occurring chaos surrounding it, make this approach mandatory. Even the best laid plans survive only the initial contact with the emergency. Adjustments have to be made and resources utilized appropriately and sometimes differently. What is done, undone or redone must be within the context of the established and prepared structure utilized by those who have trained and prepared to respond.

If you are not called, don't just go. If you are prepared to go and are called, get there in the time allotted. If you are a member of a team, follow your team guidelines. If you are not a member of a team and would like to be, check out the following and investigate others:

1. Federal Disaster Medical Assistance Teams, United States Department of Health and Human Services.
2. American Red Cross
3. Salvation Army
4. Baptist Men's Association
5. Medical Reserve Corps

6. United States Public Health Service

7. Federal Emergency Management Agency, Department of Homeland Security.

8. National Guard

9. State Defense Forces

10. Green Cross

11. Urban Search and Rescue Teams

12. United States Air Force Auxiliary, Civil Air Patrol

13. Local community teams

14. Police department auxiliaries and reserves.

15. Fire department auxiliaries

16. Community Emergency Response Teams (CERT)

17. Mental Health Teams

18. Incident Command System, Incident Management Teams

19. Special Needs Shelters

20. Medical Shelters

21. Chaplain Services (If trained to respond to disasters)

22. Disaster Relief within various denominations

A Final Note

Getting involved in a formal way requires a commitment of some kind. Doing so will allow for a better response. It will also allow for more satisfying experience for you. Certainly it will prevent many of the problems that occur when well-wishers and do-gooders show up. To really be helpful, you need to be part of the solution rather than part of the already burgeoning problem. **Don't just show up.**

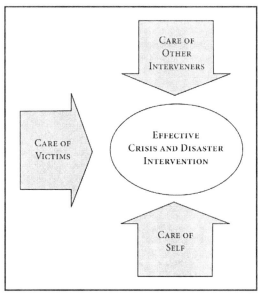

FIGURE 1.6. EFFECTIVE CRISIS AND DISASTER INTERVENTION

Chapter 10

Law and Order: SCU (Special Crisis Understanding)

**Remember and never forget:
Even responders must know and obey the law**

> Nothing stated in this chapter should be construed in any way to be legally definitive or to replace your own research into the laws of your state and city. Nor should you take this information as legal advice or as negation of the importance of seeking competent counsel from a licensed attorney.

Although Crisis Intervention and the intervener's function are not about the legalities involved, one should at least consider how these legalities relate to intervention. We live in a litigious society, where self-responsibility is often lacking and lawsuits are frequently the remedy. Lawsuits can be filed against anyone, at almost any time, and for almost any reason if a plaintiff feels that a personal wrong or injury has been caused. Generally such claims are brought under civil or tort law rather than under criminal law. That is, civil offenses (or torts) have been committed against individuals rather than against the state. Additionally, it is important to stress that ignorance of the law or of your legal responsibilities may be no defense to your actions if challenged legally.

Nothing said here can completely prevent such action or insulate the intervener or responder from all exposure. However, some guidelines, procedures, and areas of awareness can ease the potential legal burden of the intervener and allow everyone to get on with the real job of effective assistance to those in crisis.

Again, this chapter is not an inclusive list of the legalities that might arise. All interveners should be familiar with the following issues and how the laws regarding these issues apply to them. They include:

Negligence	Confidentiality
Informed consent	Exceptions to confidentiality
Duty to warn	Right to privacy
Recordkeeping	"Good Samaritan" laws
Right to refuse intervention	Abandonment
Standards of care	Consent to intervention
Altered standards of care	Actual consent
Implied consent	

To work effectively in the Crisis Intervention and Disaster Response field, interveners must recognize that they are bound by the laws of society and that, even under extreme circumstances, such proscriptions cannot be ignored without consequence. "Good Samaritan" laws generally protect those whose intent it is to assist others in times of crisis. Such assistance must always be reasonable and prudent and must be based on the level and kind of training the intervener has received and now applies. To such standards of care we must adhere.

For example, the Good Samaritan Law of the State of Texas (Chapter 74 of the Civil Practice and Remedies Code, (2007)) states that:

SUBCHAPTER D. EMERGENCY CARE

Sec. 74.151. LIABILITY FOR EMERGENCY CARE.
(a) A person who in good faith administers emergency care is not liable in civil damages for an act performed during the emergency unless the act is willfully or wantonly negligent, including a person who:

>(1) administers emergency care using an automated external defibrillator; or

>(2) administers emergency care as a volunteer who is a first responder as the term is defined under Section 421.095, Government Code.

(b) This section does not apply to care administered:

>(1) for or in expectation of remuneration, provided that being legally entitled to receive remuneration for the

emergency care rendered shall not determine whether or not the care was administered for or in anticipation of remuneration; or

(2) by a person who was at the scene of the emergency because he or a person he represents as an agent was soliciting business or seeking to perform a service for remuneration.

(c), (d) Deleted by Acts 2003, 78th Leg., ch. 204, Sec. 10.01.

(e) This section does not apply to a person whose negligent act or omission was a producing cause of the emergency for which care is being administered.

Acts 1985, 69th Leg., ch. 959, Sec. 1, eff. Sept. 1, 1985. Amended by Acts 1993, 73rd Leg., ch. 960, Sec. 1, eff. Aug. 30, 1993; Acts 1999, 76th Leg., ch. 679, Sec. 2, eff. Sept. 1, 1999. Renumbered from Sec. 74.001 and amended by Acts 2003, 78th Leg., ch. 204, Sec. 10.01, eff. Sept. 1, 2003.

Amended by:
Acts 2007, 80th Leg., R.S., Ch. 705, Sec. 1, eff. June 15, 2007.

Similar Good Samaritan laws exist in all 50 states. Interveners should be familiar with the content of the law that applies to them. It is important to ascertain if such laws actually apply to disaster responders or if other specific laws supersede good Samaritan. The following list of websites will help you find what pertains to your particular location and incident.

www.publichealthlaw.net

http://www.govtrack.us

DisasterHelp.gov

http://www.cdc.gov/phlp/publications/topic/emergency.html

www.findlaw.com

www.nolo.com

Unless an intervener has a preexisting duty to intervene in another person's crisis, the law does not require that anyone intervene in the crisis of anyone else. Police, fire fighters, and emergency service personnel usually have a preexisting duty because they are hired to perform such tasks. Further, once an intervener has begun an intervention with another person, the intervention must continue until or unless the intervener is relieved by someone with greater competency. Not to do so could be construed as abandonment and could expose the intervener to legal consequences.

Liability is generally determined by the courts; therefore, the concept of negligence, or malpractice, must be understood by all interveners. In Crisis Intervention and disaster response, good intentions are often not enough to avoid legal problems.

Negligence may result when an intervener assumes a duty of reasonable care for a victim and then breaches that duty, thereby causing damage or further injury to the victim. Generally, except when interveners have a preexisting duty, they are not required to intervene with a victim. Their moral or ethical values may dictate otherwise, however.

If an intervener, with or without a preexisting duty, decides to intervene with a sufferer, the intervener may assume a duty of reasonable care for that sufferer. Further, such a duty may be seen as assumed if the intervener acts in a way that creates a foreseeable risk to the victim.

For example, an intervener decides to take action to assist a sufferer. The action resulting from that decision creates a foreseeable risk to the victim; that is, the intervener's action could adversely affect the victim. In this case, the intervener has assumed a duty of reasonable care. If the usual procedure in this particular intervention is to remove the victim from the crisis situation, and the intervener decides against such movement, such a decision might cause additional injury to the victim.

If, as a result of such action, the victim is injured further or is damaged in other ways, the intervener may be said to have breached the duty of reasonable care and to have acted negligently. In such a case, a court might be asked to decide the intervener's liability based on the damages caused. Generally, the measure of negligence the court applies will be the guided by the standard or level of care required and given by the attending intervener. It must also be shown that the intervener's actions are the proximate or direct cause of the injury that the sufferer sustains.

Conversely, should the intervener decide not to intervene, lack of action would not create a duty of reasonable care because the intervener's actions—or inaction—would not have created risk to the victim other than that already experienced by the victim at that time. Even though inaction might allow the victim's suffering to continue, no duty of reasonable care has been created because in this case there is no duty to rescue. However, for police, fire fighters, and emergency medical service personnel, the exact opposite may be true because of their preexisting duty to act in such cases.

The following guidelines are intended to help interveners avoid the difficulties of legal confrontations and to keep them where they belong; doing what they are best trained to do serving in the field, helping victims manage the crises in their lives.

Legal and Ethical Guidelines in Crisis Intervention

1. Always treat people as human beings, not just as cases.

2. Show respect to all with whom you are involved.

3. Intervene within the limits of your background and training. Do not exceed those limits, thereby committing the illegal practice of medicine, law, or psychology.

4. Unless you have a preexisting duty to intervene, consider carefully whether you want to perform an intervention.

5. Once you have begun to intervene, don't stop.

6. Discontinue your intervention only if you are relieved by someone with greater skill than your own.

7. Determine how the Good Samaritan laws relate to the types of intervention in which you may be involved.

8. If in doubt about your legal standing, contact a competent attorney and discuss your concerns.

9. Maintain confidentiality of all information you obtain about a crisis victim. Understand under what special circumstances you may have a duty to warn another person or to otherwise breach intervener-victim confidentiality.

10. Document everything you say and do with a victim. This may assist you later if you or your procedures are challenged.

11. Maintain your competency. Update your training and credentials as required.

12. Whenever possible, obtain the victim's consent before you assist with the crisis. If in doubt, ask!

13. If emergency circumstances do not allow for actual consent by the victim, you may be able to proceed under the doctrine of implied consent. However, in such circumstances, do only what is absolutely necessary to effectively intervene or rescue.

14. Do not disturb a crime scene. If you cannot avoid doing so, note exact locations of whatever is moved so that later you can give such information to proper authorities.

15. If you must search a victim's personal effects, try to have one or two witnesses present to observe your actions.

16. Know what you are required to report to the authorities. Requirements vary from state to state. (For example, child abuse must be reported in most states.)

17. Know the legal procedures in your jurisdiction for admissions for psychiatric care. Usually admissions are categorized as either voluntary or involuntary.

18. Remember that crisis interveners and disaster responders are not usually immune from observation of motor vehicle laws or from legal responsibility for vehicular accidents or property damage.

19. Respect the victim's right to privacy. (See # 9)

20. If the victim is a minor, obtain the permission of one of the parents before intervening. If this is not possible, you may be able to proceed under the doctrine of implied consent, as you would with an adult. (See # 13)

21. Be honest and open with victims.

22. Always think through what you will do, toward what end you will be doing it, what risks are present, and what safeguards you will apply.

23. Prepare yourself with knowledge of the law as well as of Crisis Intervention skills.

24. Remember that liability can be affected by both acts of commission and acts of omission.

25. Respect a sufferer's right to refuse your intervention.

26. Before entering a crisis or disaster victim's domain, dwelling, or

office, request that person's permission. Know when the laws of your locality permit you to enter without permission.

27. If you are the director or supervisor of a Crisis Intervention agency, be sure all interveners and hotline workers understand and can apply agency policies and procedures.

28. Within Crisis Intervention agencies, develop specific, understandable policies and procedures that clearly regulate and illustrate how intervention is to be performed.

29. As an agency director or supervisor, adhere to agency policy and insist that interveners do likewise.

30. Incorporate agency policies and legal issues into the training of crisis interveners and disaster responders.

A Final Note

Know what laws apply to what you do. As more emphasis than ever is being placed on crisis and disaster response, laws, policies, and directives are being developed. While they may not always be coordinated with other existing laws, nevertheless they may apply to and affect what you do and your accountability. Do your own research. Know where you stand legally. Understand how to avoid problems before they occur if you can. Make the law work for you by understanding and appreciating it. Your work is too important not to do this. As was stated earlier, the best legal advice comes from your attorney or your organization's attorney.

LEGAL REFERENCES

Take the time to review the laws of your state. Search the internet for your state laws or use the links below. Remember, this book is not a source of legal advice, but help for you to avoid some of the pitfalls into which others have fallen. The best legal advice comes from your attorney or the attorney of your umbrella organization.

www.publichealthlaw.net

http://www.govtrack.us

http://www.archives.gov/preservation/disaster-response/

http://www.cdc.gov/phlp/publications/topic/emergency.html

www.findlaw.com

www.nolo.com

Case Law

The case law listed below has set precedents for legalities applicable to the intervener's work:

Arizona Revised Statute for Privileged Communications, § 322085 (1965). (Privileged Communications)

Buwa v. Smith, 84 1905 NMB (1986). (Duty to Warn)

Canterbury v. Spense, 464 F. 2d. 772 (D.C. Cir. 1972), cert. den. 93 S.Ct. 560 (1972). (Informed Consent)

Cutter v. Brownbridge, Cal. Ct. App., 1st Dist. 330 (1986). (Privileged Communications)

Hales v. Pittman, 118 Ariz. 305, 576 P. 2d. 493 (1978). (Informed Consent)

McDonald v. Clinger, 446 N.Y.S. 2d. 801 (1982). (Confidentiality)

McIntosh v. Milano, 403 A. 2d. 500 (N.J.S.Ct. 1979). (Duty to Warn)

New Jersey Revised Statutes, New Jersey Marriage Counseling Act, Annotated § 45: 8B 29 (1969). (Exceptions to Confidentiality)

People v. District Court, City and County of Denver, 719 P. 2d. 722 (Colo. 1986). (Privileged Communications)

Rodriguez v. Jackson, 118 Ariz. 13, 574 P. 2d. 481 (App. 1978). (Informed Consent)

Sard v. Hardy, 291 Md. 432, 379 A. 2d. 1014 (1977). (Informed Consent)

Tarasoff v. Regents of California, 131 Cal. Rptr. 14, 551 P. 2d. 334 (1976). (Duty to Warn)

Whitree v. State of New York, 56 Misc. 2d. 693, 290 N.Y.S. 2s. 486 (1968). (Record Keeping)

Chapter 11

Interpreters and Their Effective Use: Speaking the Same Language

**Remember and never forget:
Accurate communication is foremost to effective intervention**

The methods of using an interpreter during Crisis Intervention, medical, and psychological procedures with a non-English speaking patient are often compromised by lack of proper training both for primary healthcare personnel and potential interpreters, and by misunderstandings about effective procedural guidelines. Training is paramount and not everyone can do this important job. Being a fluent speaker of several languages does not in itself an interpreter make. This chapter provides specific guidelines on what may be required in order to do successful interpretation.

Introduction

Interpreters are of value only if they, or their agency, can be trusted, and if their contribution to the healthcare procedures fosters team involvement and successful patient treatment. Specific training is required to make this process work effectively.

One common mistake is allowing the interpreter to conduct the medical or behavioral health examination, the interview, or other procedures simply because they speak the language of the patient. Regardless of the language spoken and interpreted, the physician, physician's assistant, behavioral health provider or crisis intervener must conduct the actual professional interaction with the patient or crisis victim. This is true even if the interpreter happens to be a trained medical provider. Interpreters are interpreters only. The only exception might be when the healthcare or behavioral health provider is fluent in the non-English speaker's language. The problem here is that if the interaction is conducted completely in another language by the healthcare provider and the patient, the rest of the treatment team, who may not speak the alternate language, are excluded from the valuable information being transmitted and from providing their input. Primary treatment providers should not be interpreters for their own cases, and interpreters should not be primary treatment providers. Exigent circumstances may be cause to evaluate this rule.

FIGURE 11.1 – INTERPRETER, PROVIDER,
NON-ENGLISH SPEAKER ARRANGEMENT

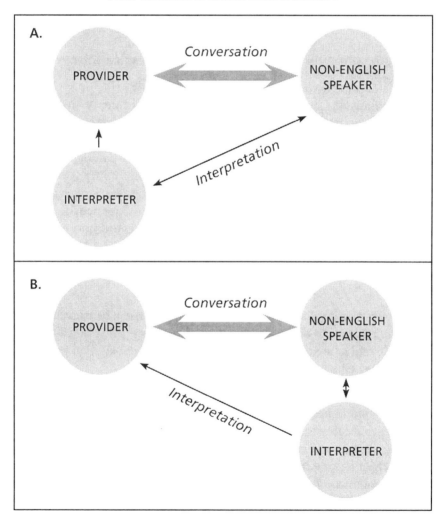

Background

The context for this material is the extensive experience of this author in the development, utilization and observation of the specific guidelines presented herein. The author's background as a police officer and as a trainer of hostage and crisis negotiators, including utilization of these procedures under hostage and barricade situations, forms a basis for what follows. Additionally, the military medical experience of the author as the Chief of Behavioral Health Services for a military Medical Brigade is significant. Also, the observations of medical provider's utilization of, and problems with, interpreters when dealing with medical and behavioral health patients, spurred the further development of this material in this context. (Greenstone, 2005 and Greenstone, 2008). This author has extensive experience with, and in the development of, Crisis Intervention training and procedures. Interpreting is an important area of concern; an area not often addressed in the context of emergency mental health and critical incidents. (Greenstone, 2010 and 2011).

Recently, this author became aware of the Certification Commission for Healthcare Interpreters. They will undoubtedly benefit the overall healthcare industry. They distinguish between interpreters and translators and are not focused on crisis or emergency situations as in this chapter. While translators and interpreters have been used in various commercial and legal venues, the novelty of this material is the specific development and utilization of interpreter practice guidelines essential in crisis, behavioral health, medical and military circumstances. (CCHI, 2010).

NB: The primary focus of this chapter is on non-English speaking patients, disaster and crisis victims, and examinees. The same presented principles are applicable in any circumstance where the provider and the sufferer or victim do not speak the same language.

Specific Guidelines Checklist

1. Interpreters must be chosen carefully prior to actual healthcare involvement. If this person can participate in training scenarios, so much the better. This will increase effectiveness and reduce initial clumsiness with the system.

2. If possible, interpreters should be recruited from reputable agencies that provide such services and have interpreters readily available and properly trained according to these guidelines. Additional training may be needed on-the-job even if the agency is reputable.

3. In the alternative to an agency, a specific person with the required skills should be sought, evaluated, and trained by the healthcare or behavioral health team.

4. The interpreter only acts as a "word machine" for the primary provider; nothing more.

5. The interpreter does not conduct the ongoing dialogue with, or examination of, the patient, victim, or examinee. The interpreter will not engage the examinee in conversation, leaving such interaction to the behavioral healthcare provider who will make all introductions and explanations to the patient. The interpreter will respond as these guidelines require.

6. Interpreters must say to the person exactly what the healthcare provider says and in the same way as the provider says it; word for word.

7. Similarly, the interpreter must say to the primary behavioral healthcare or Crisis Intervention provider exactly what the patient says and in the same way that the patient says it. No deviations are permitted.

8. Interpreters should not paraphrase what either the healthcare provider or the sufferer says. Do not say, "What he said was....," or, "What she is trying to say is..." Just repeat word-for-word what is said on either side of the conversation. If another healthcare provider joins the conversation, the same would apply for the interpreter. Let the healthcare provider interpret the patient's response and ask additional questions to clarify as needed.

9. Information about the patient's tone, inflection, cultural meanings, etc., will be given directly to the behavioral healthcare provider if such nuances may not successfully cross cultural boundaries. The interpreter should be instructed to do this by the primary healthcare provider. This is vital to the provider in order to make accurate assessments of the situation.

10. Interpreters should not add personal interpretations about what the patient or healthcare provider is saying. If asked by the healthcare provider to do so, they may provide their personal interpretations to the degree needed.

11. The interpreter should be fluent specifically in English and in the language of the non–English-speaking person. Healthcare providers

must confirm this dual fluency prior to using the interpreter. Quasi fluency in either language is unacceptable. Such lack of fluency can put the patient / sufferer and healthcare provider in jeopardy.

12. The interpreter should have no conflicts of interest that would prevent him or her from relating information accurately, or from working with the Crisis Intervention team, medical strike team or behavioral health unit in the intervention, examination and / or treatment of any patient. This must be explored before the interpreter is used.

13. When using the interpreter, the primary healthcare provider should speak in short phrases in order to allow for accurate translations. This procedure is called, "chunking." This takes practice and a little more time to do. It will be worth the effort.

14. The behavioral healthcare provider should always speak directly to the patient or victim and maintain eye contact. Be aware that eye contact is not always culturally acceptable. When speaking to the patient, do not look at the interpreter. The conversation must always be between the healthcare provider and the patient or victim even though two different languages are being used.

15. The interpreter should translate in short phrases utilizing the concept of "chunking." (See 13.)

16. The interpreter is not part of the behavioral healthcare team unless specifically needed in that capacity.

17. Remember, the interpreter only translates. Nothing more.

18. These same procedures are easily adaptable to telephone interactions with non-English speakers. For telephone translations, a secondary phone line attached to the primary phone will be needed so that the interpreter can hear both sides of the conversation. The interpreter should sit near the healthcare provider who is on the phone with the patient or victim to facilitate the transfer of information.

19. Interpreters should not be used in situations within which they may feel uncomfortable or threatened. Such concerns may compromise the translations and the meaningfulness of the healthcare provider / patient interactions.

20. If you have concerns regarding the accuracy of an interpreter or of a translation, have the interaction verified by another person fluent

in both languages, or by another bona fide, appropriately trained, interpreter.

21. The behavioral healthcare provider should confirm the victim's ability to speak English. This can be done by checking with others who may know the victim or merely by speaking to the victim in English. If the patient or victim speaks at least some English, communicate directly in English, and have the interpreter stand-by to assist if needed.

22. Speaking with someone who only speaks some or minimal English will tend to slow down the conversation and examination. It may also provide for added accuracy because the patient or examinee or victim must consider their responses more carefully before speaking.

23. Interpreters must convey to the behavioral healthcare provider idiomatic nuances in the verbal exchanges that may not be obvious to the listener. This should be done directly to the provider or intervener.

24. The interpreter should not insert his or her own beliefs or possible alternative approaches to the victim's problems or difficulties. This may be more of a problem for an interpreter with more experience. Resist the temptation. (See 17.)

25. The interpreter should not editorialize or express personal opinions or emotions except as requested by the behavioral healthcare provider; never to the patient or victim. (DiVasto, 1996). (See 17.)

26. It is good practice for the interpreter to have a small note pad and pen or pencil available to them throughout the interaction. A pad, such as a journalist's notebook, may work well.

27. The interpreter should use the small notepad only to capture those items spoken by either the behavioral health provider or the patient that may be too long in content for the interpreter to remember. It is important that all information be transmitted. The occasional use of the notepad may help in this regard.

28. As seen in Figure 11.1, the arrangement of interpreter, provider and patient or victim may be set differently depending on the circumstances that exist at the time. Flexibility is important to make this process work at optimal levels.

29. Interpreters should interpret exclamations from the patient or provider in the way that they are presented. For example, if the patient or victim exclaims, "Ouch" in their language, the interpreter should repeat the exclamation in English with the same emotional level used by the patient.

30. An experienced interpreter may be able to do ongoing interpretation as either the provider or victim / patient is talking. This takes practice. The interpreter may have to sit closer to the provider or victim and speak in a lower volume so that the conversation between them is not interrupted. The provider may give guidance to the interpreter about how this is to be done.

Printable checklist in Appendix A, page 162.

Final Note

Do not underestimate the power, importance and impact of these procedures in developing the needed relationship between the behavioral healthcare provider or intervener and the patient. It is possible to carry on in-depth conversations just as one would if all parties were speaking the same language. Such abilities will allow for the highest level of intervention and victim care.

Chapter 12

A History of the Crisis Intervention Movement and Discipline

Remember and never forget:
"...Those who cannot remember the past are condemned to repeat it." (Santayana, 1905)

To know where you are going, it is important to know where you have been. History is more important than we may believe. The above quote from the poet Santayana says it best. Organizations and procedures that address crises have existed since the early 1900's and even before. As far back as the 1700's, we knew of trauma-related stress conditions and referred to them by such names as, "Soldier's Heart," and later as "Combat Fatigue," "Combat Exhaustion," and similar monikers. As a result of unusually high stress brought on by certain events that may occur without warning and in a sudden fashion, a person may experience an inability to cope with life in the way he or she would under more normal conditions. Rape, natural disasters, community emergencies, personal disputes, suicide, shootings, loss of life, death of children, man-made disasters and the like can each produce sufficient stress to interrupt usual life processes and to create a crisis. From early times, emergency responders have come forth from various sectors and with varying degrees of skill, and with various ideas, in an attempt to address this important phenomenon. In many instances, these procedures and organizations were loosely organized and trained in a variety of ways and to various degrees.

Crisis intervention and later the discipline of Crisis Intervention were set in motion by the early studies of the victims of man-made disasters and families affected by wartime deaths. As techniques developed, they were applied to many diverse fields, including law enforcement, penology, social service, business, religion and nursing. Many definitions of Crisis Intervention appeared and, as the term gained professional acceptance, books and papers were written under this popular heading. They covered topics from psychotherapeutic techniques to short term therapy. All in all, Crisis Intervention was not well regarded as other than an adjunct to other more standardized disciplines. Today, "crisis" and "intervention" as well as "crisis management" have become part of common parlance to mean many things other than the concepts discussed in this book. We hear of a crisis in the White House, a crisis in Iran, a crisis in health care. Crisis Management meant handling, in one way or another, whatever difficulty presented itself, and had no recognized professional place of its own. Academic institutions had trouble with the concept and it was not until years later that such courses were offered for actual academic study and academic credit. For many years, it was thought that good counselors also made good crisis interveners; perhaps by osmosis or by other theoretical mumbo-jumbo. Of course, we know that this is not the actual case in practice.

It took some years and persistent advocacy to make the point that psychotherapeutic experience does not in itself supply Crisis Intervention expertise. In order to fully understand crises and intervention into such situations, specific definitions, procedures and training are essential. Crisis Intervention needed to be recognized as a professional discipline with a tradition, a definite place in today's professional and paraprofessional community and a future within the overall behavioral health care system. It must have its own professionals, organizations, training academies, certifications, journals and recognition to allow its development as a significant and viable scientific entity.

A complete history of the movement is an important subject for another book (See Hotline: Crisis Intervention Directory, 1981) There is value in discussing the genesis of the decision by this author and others to spend succeeding years doing the groundwork necessary to help establish Crisis Intervention as a viable discipline.

In the late 1950's and early 1960's plans and procedures were developed by Rosenbluh and others that operationalized and formalized a fledgling discipline. In 1969, The Southern Indiana Chapter of the National Conference of Christians and Jews began a project in Louisville, Kentucky designed to provide training in community relations and Crisis Intervention. As it developed, the project gave professionals, paraprofessionals and nonprofessionals training and experience in techniques of crisis management that could prevent crisis related emotional upsets from becoming disastrous to the people involved. A few years later, an offshoot of this initial program was established to show that Crisis Intervention procedures and principles could be applied to any crisis situation. The methods used by police officers were found to be applicable and highly useful to crisis center counselors and vice verse. The major proponents of this interdisciplinary approach were Dr. Edward S. Rosenbluh and this author, who began piecing it together while completing their professional training. Lieutenant James E. Oney of the Louisville Division of Police, and Dr. Kent A. Rensin, a former police officer and high school administrator were early members. Dr. Sharon Leviton soon joined the team along with Dr. W. Rodney Fowler.

From these beginnings, the National Institute for Training in Crisis Intervention emerged. There, on a regularly scheduled basis, students of Crisis Management, regardless of professional credentials, could receive specific and expert training. The National Institute laid the groundwork in 1976 for the formation of the American Academy of Crisis Interveners. This Academy served as the first national attempt to unify and organize the field of Crisis Intervention. Professional recognition and identity for crisis workers was now assured. The Southwestern Academy of Crisis Interveners was formed in 1978 with Dr. Sharon C. Leviton as its Executive Director. The Southeastern Academy formed shortly afterward by Dr. W. Rodney Fowler. Dr. Fowler is a Distinguished Professor at the University of Tennessee at Chattanooga and introduced Crisis Intervention training into the academic counseling program at his university. Subsequently, the National Training Conference for Crisis Intervention developed and offered multiple levels of training including Basic, Intermediate and Advanced Crisis Intervention training. Following this, a certification program was established to allow any crisis worker who qualified to be certified within his/her own discipline. All training adhered to the interdisciplinary concept that permits not only the needed social interaction among agencies, but also the sharing of their skills to the mutual benefit of all. To further these efforts again, the American Board of Examiners in Crisis Intervention was formed in 1980.

The alliance in 2002 of The American College of Forensic Examiners International (ACFEI) and the American Board of Examiners in Crisis Intervention (ABECI) was welcomed by those who labored for years to advance Crisis Intervention as a discipline of its own.

Certification is certainly one marker of accomplishment and success. To have passed the written, the oral, and the practical portions of the exam along with submitting an original paper suitable for publication is an important and distinguished accomplishment. Other markers include participating in ongoing team training, studying, publishing, and taking personal responsibility for being prepared physically and emotionally to intervene. Being aware and being prepared speaks to how seriously an intervener takes his/her profession. We learned from the past and moved forward with vigor. It is very hard to know where you are going, however, if you do not know from whence you cometh. The discipline of Crisis Intervention moved forward. Development occurred, and continues to occur, in many important areas including disaster response and emergency preparedness.

A Final Note

Now you know a little about the history of Crisis Intervention.

A complete history of the Crisis Intervention movement in the United States is not appropriate in this particular *Field Guide*. However, interveners are encouraged to search out and examine the various groups and services that have developed over the years both during and after what has been described above, and those mentioned elsewhere in this *Field Guide*. Also, note well the work of Green Cross, The International Critical Incident Stress Foundation, the American Association of Experts in Traumatic Stress, the American Mental Health Counselors Association, and the Military Emergency Management Specialist Qualification of the State Guard Association of the United States. Undoubtedly others will emerge as you continue your perusal.

Appendix A – Forms and Charts

You may photocopy the contents of Appendix A.
A digital download is available from Whole Person Associates containing
a PDF file that includes all of Appendix A for easy printing.
This may not be purchased unless you have/are purchasing the book.
Call Whole Person Associates at 800-247-6789 to order your download or
you can find it on the website at the bottom of the Emotional First Aid page.

FIGURE 1.1. PSYCHOLOGICAL STRUCTURING, CHAPTER 1, PAGE 2.
External and internal factors in an external stimulus situation.
(Sherif and Sherif, 1956)

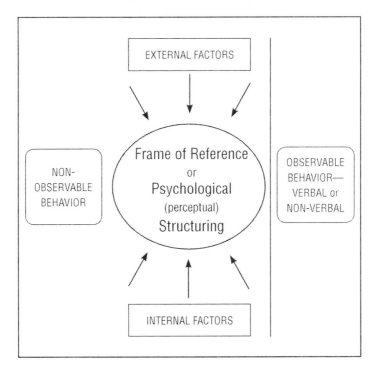

External Factors	Internal Factors
Objects	Motives
Cultural products	Attitudes
Person	Emotions
Groups	Various states of the organism
	Effects of past experiences

(Continued on the next page)

FIGURE 1.1. PSYCHOLOGICAL STRUCTURING (*Continued*)

Additionally, Sherif and Sherif (1948 and 1956) provided their basic and unyielding principles of social interaction that provide a background for our understanding of Crises and Emotional First Aid. The following are adaptations of these remarkable principles that Sherif believed apply in all social situations. The implications for understanding and for responding effectively to those in crisis can be easily seen. What we do is based on what we know about what the sufferer or victim is doing, thinking or experiencing.

1. Experience and behavior constitute a unity.
2. Behavior follows central psychological structuring. See Figure 1.1.
3. Psychological structuring is jointly determined by external and internal factors. See Figure 1.1.
4. Internal factors such as motives, attitudes, etc. and experience are inferred from behavior.
5. The psychological tendency is toward structuring of experience.
6. Structured stimulus situations set limits to alternatives in psychological structuring.
7. In unstructured stimulus situations, alternatives in psychological structuring are increased.
8. The more unstructured the stimulus situation, the greater the relative contribution of internal factors in the frame of reference.
9. The more unstructured the stimulus situation, the greater the relative contribution of external social factors in the frame of reference.
10. Various factors in the frame of reference have differing relative weights.
11. Psychological activity is selective.
12. Human psychological functioning is typically on the conceptual level. (Sherif and Sherif, 1948 and 1956).

FIGURE 1.2 – THE CRISIS CUBE, CHAPTER 1, PAGE 4

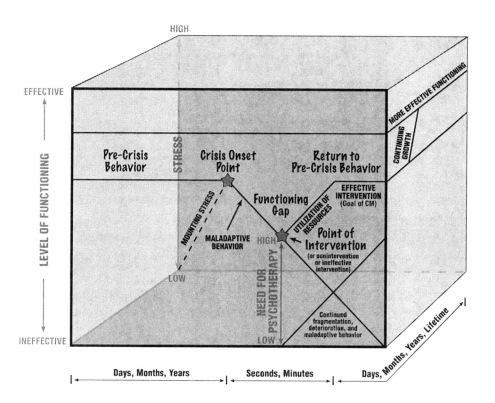

FIGURE 1.3 –CRISIS VS CRISIS MANAGEMENT, CHAPTER 1, PAGE 5
How crises tend to emotionally shut down sufferers and how effective
crisis management and emotional first aid can reverse the process.
(Adapted form Evarts, Greenstone, et al, 1983)

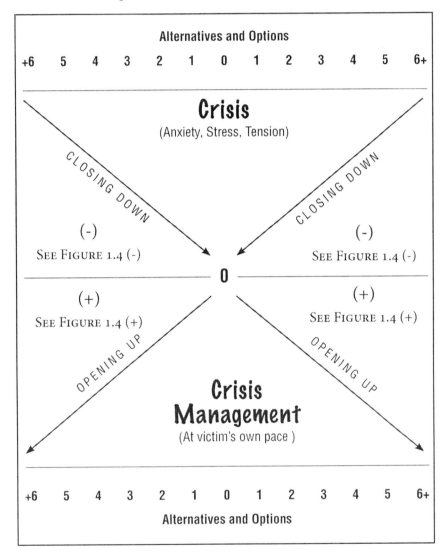

FIGURE 1.4. THE ELEMENTS OF CRISIS VS CRISIS MANAGEMENT,
CHAPTER 1, PAGE 6

What happens during crisis (-)	What happens during crisis management or crisis intervention (+)
Tendency to close down emotionally.	Tendency to open up at sufferer's own pace.
Access to resources decreases.	Maladaptive behavior decreases.
Supports more difficult to access or unavailable.	Resource utilization increases.
Problem-solving ability decreases.	Problem solving skills increase.
Maladaptive behavior increases.	Access to or recognition of support systems increase.
Psychological growth is limited.	Possibilities for growth increase.
Possibility of physical violence escalates.	Chances of physical violence decrease.
Pre-crisis behavior inaccessible.	Likelihood of returning to pre-crisis behavior increases.
Difficulty seeing helpful possibilities.	Ability to get on with one's life increases.
Interactions close down.	Opens interactions with others.
Threats may increase.	Reduction in feelings of frustration.
Higher levels of frustration.	Decrease in threats.
Alternatives seem limited. (*After the crisis*)	Alternatives open up and can be recognized. (*After the crisis*)
Options seem limited. (*During the crisis*)	Options more readily available. (*When dealing with the crisis*)

FIGURE 1.5 – THE CRISIS CONTINUUM, CHAPTER 1, PAGE 7

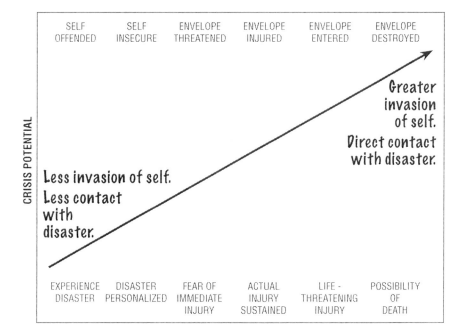

FIGURE 1.6– EFFECTIVE CRISIS AND DISASTER INTERVENTION,
CHAPTER 1, PAGE 9
To remain helpful, we must remain effective.

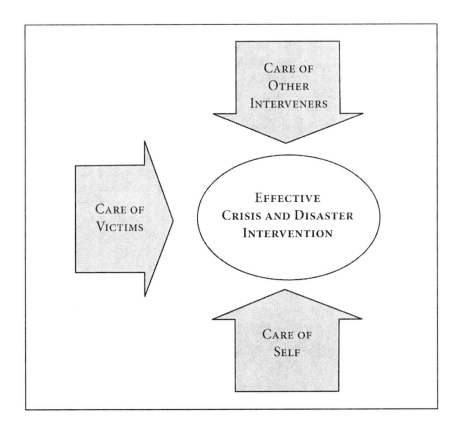

Figure 2.1 – CRISIS INTERVENTION MODEL FOR RESPONSE,
CHAPTER 2, PAGE 11
(Greenstone and Leviton, 1982)

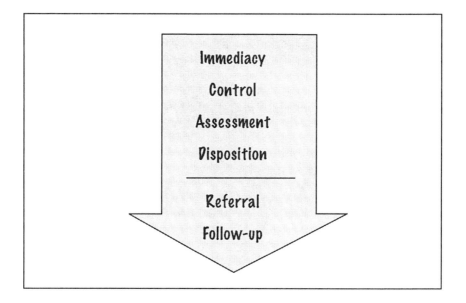

FIG. 2.2 – CRISIS CASUALTY RESPONSE CHART, CHAPTER 2, PAGE 15
Print this page and keep it in the front of your Crisis Intervention Notebook.

While victim is still involved	Care after removal of victim from crisis situation	Evacuation: Medivac vs. Emotional First Aid Evacuation
Expect that a crisis victim may stay involved within the crisis situation … e.g. continue to clear rubble from their destroyed house.	Assess altered mental status.	Specify best route in to location.
Work alongside the crisis victim as needed.	Perform physical first aid as needed.	Radio – specify channels or frequencies.
Keep self out of harm's way.	Airway establishment.	Specify number of patients to be evacuated and precedence.
Keep victim from additional or greater stress if possible.	Breathing checked.	Medical.
Expect the sufferer's stress level may increase.	Bleeding stopped.	Immediate.
Attend to minor physical wounds.	Splint broken bones.	Delayed.
Prevent additional physical wounds.	Communicate with victim.	Minor.
Stop any life threatening behavior.	Cardiopulmonary resuscitation as needed.	Extreme.
Maintain appropriate communication with sufferers.	Check wounds.	Specify equipment needed.
Explain your actions to the sufferer.	Get victim to medical clearing as soon as possible as needed.	Specify how many victims are ambulatory.
Reassure realistically.	The "ABC's" of Emotional First Aid: Begin Emotional First Aid immediately.	Specify how many victims are on litters.
Remove victim from crisis situation if additional emotional or physical injury may occur.	A = Assessment and control B = Begin emotional first aid C = Clear sufferer to definitive care	Describe security at pick-up site and inform them of the pending arrival of evacuation personnel and vehicles.
Evacuate as appropriate to definitive care.	Assessment and control— Begin Emotional First Aid— Clear to care	Describe the method of marking the pick-up site.
Stay hydrated.	Fluids as needed.	Describe the contamination, if any.
Help victim stay hydrated.	Reassure victims realistically.	None.
Other concerns, Notes, Lists.		Emotional First Aid only.
		Nuclear.
		Biological.
		Chemical.

FIGURE 2.3 – HYDRATION CHART. ENGLISH.

Hydration for self and victim by checking urine coloration.

Clear
Good hydration level.
Drink 1 quart H2O over next 120 minutes.

Light Yellow
Adequate hydration level.
Drink 1 quart H2O over next 60 minutes.

Yellow
Low hydration level.
Drink 1 quart H2O in next 30 minutes.

Dark Yellow
Very low hydration level.
Drink 1 quart H2O in next 15 minutes.

Dark Yellow – Orange
Dangerously low hydration level.
Drink at least 1 quart H2O ASAP.

FIGURE 2.3A – HYDRATION CHART. SPANISH.
HYDRATION – Guia a higradarse.

Amarillo Oscuro – Anaranjado
Peligrosamente bajo nivel de hidratacion.
Toma por lo menos 1 cuarto de agua en seguida.

Amarillo Oscuro
Nivel muy bajo de hidratacion.
Toma por lo menos 1 cuarto de agua en 15 minutos.

Amarillo
Nivel bajo de hidratacion.
Toma por lo menos 1 cuarto de agua en 30 minutos.

Amarilloso
Nivel adecuado de hidratacion.
Toma por lo menos 1 cuarto de agua en 60 minutos.

Claro
Buen nivel de hidratacion.
Toma por lo menos 1 cuarto de agua en 120 minutos.

FIGURE 2.4

FLUID REPLACEMENT GUIDELINES FOR WARM WEATHER TRAINING
Applies to Average Acclimated Member Wearing Hot Weather Uniform

Heat Category	WBGT Index	Easy Work		Moderate Work		Hard Work	
	Intake Qt/Hr	Work/ Rest Min	Water Intake Qt/Hr	Work/ Rest Min	Water Intake Qt/Hr	Work/ Rest Min	Water Intake Qt/Hr
1	78-81.9	NL	½	NL	¾	40/20	3/4
2 (Green)	82-84.9	NL	½	50/10	¾	30/30	1
3 (Yellow)	85-87.9	NL	¾	40/20	¾	30/30	1
4 (Red)	88-89.9	NL	¾	30/30	¾	20/40	1
5 (Black)	> 90	50/10	1	20/40	1	10/50	1

- The work / rest times and fluid replacement volumes will sustain performance and hydration for at least 4 hours of work in the specified heat category. Individual water needs will vary ¼ quart / hour.
- NL = no limit to work time per hour.
- Rest means minimal physical activity (sitting or standing) accomplished in shade, if possible.
- CAUTION: Hourly fluid intake should not exceed 1 1/4 quarts.
- Daily fluid intake should not exceed 12 liters.
- Wearing body armor adds 5 degrees F to WBGT Index.
- Wearing all MOPP over-garments adds 10 degrees F to WBGT Index.

Easy Work	**Moderate Work**	**Hard Work**
Weapon Maintenance	Walking loose sand at 2.5 mph, no load	Walking hard surface at 3.5 mph with a 50 pound load
Walking hard surface at 2.5 mph, with a 30 pound load	Walking hard surface at .5 mph with a 40 pound load	Walking on loose sand at 2.5 mph with load
Guard Duty	Calisthenics	Field assaults
Marksmanship training	Patrolling	
Drill and ceremony	Individual movement techniques such as low crawl, high crawl	*Source: FM 21-10*
	Defensive position construction	*Field Sanitation*

FIG. 3.1 – WHAT CRISIS INTERVENERS DO, CHAPTER 3, PAGE 17

- Question sufferer cogently.
- Observe victim keenly.
- Listen carefully to sufferer.
- Think deeply about the victim's problems.
- Think as a crisis intervener.
- Statistics cannot substitute for the sufferer before you.
- Victims can help interveners think.

FIGURE. 3.2 – CRISIS INTERVENTION
and DISASTER CRISIS INTERVENTION
CHAPTER 3, PAGE 18

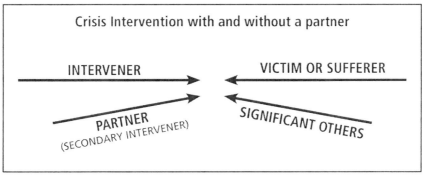

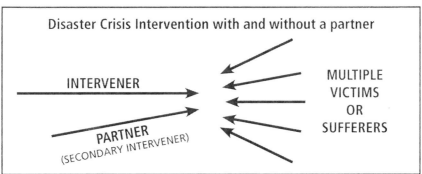

FIGURE. 3.3
CRISIS INTERVENTION TRIAGE SYSTEM
CHAPTER 3, PAGE 20

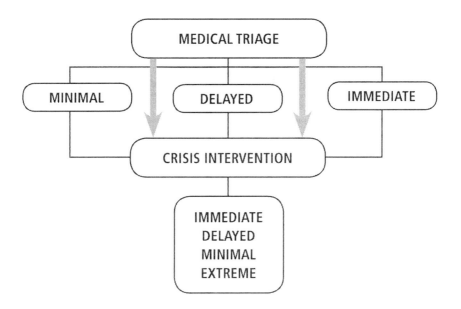

FIGURE 3.4 – TRIAGE CARD, PART 1, SIDE 1, CHAPTER 3, PAGE 22
To be attached to the crisis victim.

Name		Last 4 SS#
4 – EXTREME (BLACK) Complete emotional shutdown; Severe mental illness		
To: CARE	Location:	Behavioral Health
1 – IMMEDIATE (RED) Serious crisis that requires and will respond to STAT intervention		
To: CRISIS INTERVENTION	Location:	Behavioral Health
2 – DELAYED (YELLOW) Experiencing crisis but can wait until IMMEDIATE are seen		
To: GROUP	Location:	Behavioral Health
3 – MINIMAL (GREEN) Experiencing post trauma stress, but with some intact coping skills		
To: REST AREA or ASSIST __R __A	Location:	Behavioral Health

FIGURE 3.4 – TRIAGE CARD, PART 1, SIDE 2, CHAPTER 3, PAGE 23

Basic Overview of the Four Levels of Triage

The Disaster Crisis Intervention Triage System presented here consists of four levels of triage. This is similar to many of the emergency medical triage systems.

MINIMAL LEVEL

Few indicators of crisis. Upset and / or experiencing effects of psychosocial trauma with few or no indicators of crisis, as indicated by some of the following:
1. Coherent thought processes.
2. Able to make personal care decisions.
3. Upset or crying but obviously in control of self.
4. Able and willing to discuss experience.
5. No violent acting out behavior.
6. May want to help others.
7. Re-triage may be needed.

IMMEDIATE LEVEL

Must be seen and attended to now! In crisis as indicated by some of the following:
1. Becoming more and more depressed.
2. Out-of-structure (control issues).
3. Acting out behavior.
4. Difficulty following instructions.
5. Poor decision making.
6. Yelling and screaming.

DELAYED LEVEL

Can wait. Must be re-triaged. Very upset but obviously coping to some degree as indicated by some of the following:
1. Some withdrawal.
2. Some confusion.
3. No acting out behavior.
4. Intact decision making.
5. Expression of concerns and desire to talk to someone.

EXTREME LEVEL

Return to these only when others are assisted. May need to re-triage later as time and resources permit. These will require long-term support or psychotherapy and are not likely to respond to Crisis Intervention techniques as indicated by some of, but not limited to, the following:
1. Chronic mental illness without appropriate medications.
2. Totally unresponsive to inquiries.
3. Communication shut-down.
4. Unable to do anything for self.
5. Custodial care probably required.

FIGURE 3.5 – TRIAGE CARD, PART 2, CHAPTER 3, PAGE 24
To be attached to the crisis victim.

Name		Last 4 SS#
4 – EXTREME (BLACK)		
To: CARE	Location:	Behavioral Health
1 – IMMEDIATE (RED)		
To: CRISIS INTERVENTION	Location:	Behavioral Health
2 – DELAYED (YELLOW)		
To: GROUP	Location:	Behavioral Health
3 – MINIMAL (GREEN)		
To: REST AREA or ASSIST __R __A	Location:	Behavioral Health

FIGURE 3.6 MILITARY ACUTE CONCUSSION EVALUATION (MACE)

Military Acute Concussion Evaluation (MACE)

Patient Name: _____

SS#: _____-_____-_____   Unit: _____

Date of Injury: _____/_____/_____   Time of Injury: _____

Examiner: _____

Date of Evaluation: _____/_____/_____   Time of Evaluation: _____

History: (I – VIII)

I. Description of Incident. Ask:

a) What happened? _____

_____

_____

b) Tell me what you remember. _____

_____

_____

c) Were you dazed, confused, "saw stars"?   Yes_____   No_____

d) Did you hit your head?   Yes_____   No_____

II. Cause of Injury. (Circle all that apply):

      1)Explosion / Blast   4) Fragment

      2) Blunt object   5) Fall

      3) Motor Vehicle Crash   6) Gunshot wound

      7) Other

III. Was a helmet worn?   Yes_____   No_____   Type _____

IV. Amnesia Before. Are there any events just BEFORE the injury that are not remembered? (Assess for continuous memory prior to injury.)

Yes_____   How long? _____

© 2016 WHOLE PERSON ASSOCIATES, 101 WEST 2ND ST., SUITE 203, DULUTH MN 55802 ▪ 800·247·6789

V. Amnesia After. Are there any events just AFTER the injuries that are not remembered? (Assess time until continuous memory after the injury.)

Yes_____   How long? _____   No_____

VI. Does the individual report loss of consciousness or "blacking out?"

Yes_____   How long? _____   No_____

VII. Did anyone observe a period of loss of consciousness or unresponsiveness?

Yes_____   How long? _____   No_____

VIII. Symptoms. (Circle all that apply.)

1) Headache	6) Difficulty Concentrating
2) Dizziness	7) Irritability
3) Memory Problems	8) Visual Disturbances
4) Balance problems	9) Ringing in the ears
5) Nausea/Vomiting	10) Other _____

**Examination: (IX – XIII) Evaluate each domain.
Total possible score is 30.**

IX. Orientation. (1 point each)

Month:	0	1
Date:	0	1
Day of Week:	0	1
Year:	0	1
Time:	0	1

Orientation Total Score _____ / 5

X. Immediate Memory. Read all 5 words and ask the patient to recall them in any order. Repeat two more times for a total of three trials.

ELBOW

APPLE

CARPET

SADDLE

BUBBLE

(1 point for each correct, total over 3 trials)

Trial 1			Trial 2			Trial 3		
Elbow	0	1	Elbow	0	1	Elbow	0	1
Apple	0	1	Apple	0	1	Apple	0	1
Carpet	0	1	Carpet	0	1	Carpet	0	1
Saddle	0	1	Saddle	0	1	Saddle	0	1
Bubble	0	1	Bubble	0	1	Bubble	0	1

Trial 1 Score _____   Trial 2 Score _____   Trial 3 Score _____

Immediate Memory Total Score (Trials 1+2+3) _____ /15

XI. Neurological Screening. As the clinical condition permits, check:

Eyes: pupillary response and tracking

Verbal: speech fluency and word finding

Motor: pronator drift, gait / coordination

Record any abnormalities. _____

_____

_____

No points are given for this.

XII. Concentration: Reverse Digits. (Go to next string length if correct on first trial. Stop if incorrect on both trials.) 1 pt. for each string length.

4-9-3	0	1	6-2-9	0	1
3-8-1-4	0	1	3-2-7-9	0	1
6-2-9-7-1	0	1	1-5-2-8-5	0	1
7-1-8-4-6-2	0	1	5-3-9-1-4-8	0	1

Months in reverse order: (1 pt. for entire sequence correct)

Dec-Nov-Oct-Sep-Aug-Jul Jun-May-Apr-Mar-Feb-Jan   0   1

Concentration Total Score _____ / 5

XIII. Delayed Recall. (1 pt. each) Ask the patient to recall the 5 words from the earlier memory test (Do NOT reread the word list.)

Elbow 0 1 Apple 0 1 Carpet 0 1 Saddle 0 1 Bubble 0 1

Delayed Recall Total Score _____ /5

TOTAL SCORE _____ /30

Notes:

_____

_____

_____

_____

_____

_____

_____

Diagnosis: (circle one or write in diagnoses if known)

No concussion

850.0 Concussion without Loss of Consciousness (LOC)

850.1 Concussion with Loss of Consciousness (LOC)

Other diagnoses _____

_____

_____

_____

McCrea, M., Kelly, J. & Randolph, C. (2000).

Standardized Assessment of Concussion (SAC): Manual for Administration, Scoring, and Interpretation. (2nd ed.) Waukesa, WI: Authors.

Defense & Veterans Brain Injury Center
1-800-870-9244 or DSN: 662-6345

FIGURE 3.7 WAR EXPERIENCES INVENTORY

War Experiences Inventory and Scoring
by Katz, Et Al.

These are some common events that can happen during war. Please answer if each item happened to you by circling either "Yes" or "No." Then, for the items you answered "Yes" rate how distressing the event was for you using the following scale:

1 = Not at all   2 = Slightly   3 = Somewhat,
4 = Considerably   5 = Extremely

No   Yes _____   1. Did you experience being in firefights or bombings?

No   Yes _____   2. Did you witness others injured or killed?

No   Yes _____   3. Did you kill or injure others?

No   Yes _____   4. Were you in a difficult or dangerous situation where you felt fearful for your life?

No   Yes _____   5. Did you have friends that died in the war?

No   Yes _____   6. Did you participate in or witness violence to civilians?

No   Yes _____   7. Did you participate in or witness others inflict unnecessary brutality?

No   Yes _____   8. Did you witness human suffering?

No   Yes _____   9. Did you make, or did you witness others make a mistake that lost lives or seriously injured others?

No   Yes _____   10. Did you experience unwanted verbal comments of a sexual nature (pressure for dates, or threats)?

No   Yes _____   11. Did you experience unwanted physical sexual advances (touching, grabbing, or cornering)?

No   Yes _____   12. Were you sexually assaulted, experienced attempted or completed rape (forced or agreed to sex out of fear)?

No   Yes _____   13. Were you held at gunpoint or taken hostage?

No   Yes _____   14. Did you feel unsafe with your peers (fear they would harm you or they would not protect you)?

No   Yes _____   15. Were you treated poorly by your commanding officers?

No   Yes _____   16. Were you treated poorly by your family, friends, or the civilian population upon returning from war?

No   Yes _____   17. Were you treated poorly by your unit upon returning from war?

No   Yes _____   18. Were you injured?

No   Yes _____   19. Do you have chronic pain or disfigurement from an injury?

No   Yes _____   20. Did you witness dead bodies, severe injuries, or something grotesque?

No   Yes _____   21. Did you feel you were not well prepared to serve in this war?

No   Yes _____   22. Did you feel your peers were not well prepared to serve in this war?

No   Yes _____   23. Was there anyone in your unit who made your life difficult, stressful, or unsafe?

No   Yes _____   24. Did you feel alone, like there was nobody you could trust or go to if you had problems?

No   Yes _____   25. Did you find one or many of your superiors were incompetent, poor leaders, or not well-trained?

No   Yes _____   26. Did you deploy with relationship or family problems?

No   Yes _____   27. Did you deploy with financial problems?

No   Yes _____   28. While deployed were you concerned about things at home (e.g., your marriage, health of a family member, or job)?

No   Yes _____   29. Were you exposed to potentially harmful substances (e.g., pesticides, chemicals, or biological weapons)?

Scoring

Frequency total is the sum of the number of items with ratings of "Yes." *Severity total* is the sum of severity ratings of all items. Subscale scores are calculated as the sum of the following: *Combat exposure* (10 items) = 1, 2, 3, 4, 5, 6, 7, 8, 9, 20; *Interpersonal distress* (8 items) = 14, 15, 17, 21, 22, 23, 24, 25; *Circumstances of deployment* (3 items) = 26, 27, 28; Personal injury (3 items) = 18, 19, 29; and *Sexual trauma* (4 items) = 10, 11, 12, 13. Note: Item 16 is not included in any Subscales.

Reference

Lori S. Katz, Geta Cojucar, Cory Davenport, Satish Clarke & John C. Williams (2012): War Experiences Inventory: Initial Psychometric and Structural Properties, Military Psychology, 24:1, 48-70

To link to this article: http://dx.doi.org/10.1080/08995605.2012.642291

FIGURE 3.8 DEATH NOTIFICATION – SURVIVOR INTAKE FORM

CONFIDENTIAL INFORMATION

Information about survivors and their wishes – to be completed by the person making notification. This form is to be filled out at the time of notification and retained by the person making notification.

Name of survivor _____

Address of survivor _____

Community _____ Zip Code _____

Telephone: Home _____ Work _____

          Cell _____

Relation to the deceased _____

Name of funeral home to which the body of deceased should be sent

_____

If the survivor has no preference about funeral homes, would he or she like the medical examiner to choose one?   YES_____   NO_____

Do any survivors wish to see the body of the person who has died?
YES _____ NO_____ Will decide later _____

Are there any special items that might have been in the possession of the person who died (such as jewelry or a donor card)? List: _____

_____

_____

Others to be contacted by person making notification (other kin, unmarried partners, roommates, etc.):

_____ Phone _____

_____ Phone _____

Persons contacted by person making notification to provide support to the survivor:

_____ Phone _____

_____ Phone _____

Signature of person making notification _____

FIGURE 3.9 MENTAL STATUS

Mental Status Evaluation

Name of Intervener / Evaluator _____

Name of Victim: _____

Age _____ DOB _____ Race _____ Gender _____

Phone _____

Affect:	a) broad (WNL) e) inappropriate	b) restricted f) labile	c) blunted	d) flat
Speech:	a) normal e) slurred	b) delayed f) excessive	c) soft g) pressured	d) loud h) incoherent
Mood:	a) Euthymic (WNL) e) dysphoric	b) elevated f) irritable	c) euphoric	d) expansive
Thought Content:	a) WNL	b) delusions	c) thought insertion	d) hallucinations
Judgment:	a) intact	b) minimal impairment	c) moderate impairment	d) severe impairment
Insight:	a) intact	b) minimal impairment	c) moderate impairment	d) severe impairment
Memory:	a) intact	b) impaired recent	c) impaired remote	d) amnesic
Impulse Control / Risk Management:	a) normal	b) disciplined	c) spontaneous	d) impetuous
Attention / Concentration:	a) normal	b) difficulty finishing tasks	c) distracted	d) difficulty concentrating
Orientation:	a) fully oriented	b) disoriented x time	c) disoriented x place	d) disoriented x person
Appearance:	a) WNL	b) inappropriate	c) disheveled	d) bizarre
Attitude:	a) cooperative	b) guarded	c) suspicious	d) belligerent

(Continued on the next page)

Impression / Diagnosis

Axis I _____

_____

Axis II _____

_____

Axis III _____

_____

Axis IV _____

_____

Prognosis

Strengths _____

_____

Limitations _____

_____

Risk Level _____

_____

Recommendations _____

_____

_____

Plan of Action _____

_____

_____

_____

_____

FIGURE 3.10 MODIFIED MINI SCREEN (MMS)

Modified Mini Screen (MMS)

Client Name: _____ ID: _____

Interviewer: _____

Today's Date: _____ Initials (Optional) _____

SECTION A

YES NO 1. Have you been consistently depressed or down, most of the day, nearly every day, for the past 2 weeks?

YES NO 2. In the past 2 weeks, have you been less interested in most things or less able to enjoy the things you used to enjoy most of the time?

YES NO 3. Have you felt sad, low or depressed most of the time for the last two years?

YES NO 4. In the past month, did you think that you would be better off dead or wish you were dead?

YES NO 5. Have you ever had a period of time when you were feeling up, hyper or so full of energy or full of yourself that you got into trouble or that other people thought you were not your usual self? (Do not consider times when you were intoxicated on drugs or alcohol.)

YES NO 6. Have you ever been so irritable, grouchy or annoyed for several days, that you had arguments, verbal or physical fights, or shouted at people outside your family? Have you or others noticed that you have been more irritable or overreacted, compared to other people, even when you thought you were right to act this way?

_____ Total number of YES responses to questions 1–6, Section A

SECTION B

YES NO 7. *Note: This question is in two parts. If the answer to BOTH a and b is YES, code the question YES. If the answer to either or both a and b is NO, code the question NO.*

(Continued on the next page)

YES   NO   a. Have you had one or more occasions when you felt intensely anxious, frightened, uncomfortable or uneasy even when most people would not feel that way?

YES   NO   b. If yes, did these intense feelings get to be their worst within 10 minutes?

YES   NO   8. Do you feel anxious or uneasy in places or situations where you might have the panic-like symptoms we just spoke about? Or do you feel anxious or uneasy in situations where help might not be available or escape might be difficult? Examples include:
- ❏ Being in a crowd
- ❏ Standing in a line
- ❏ Being alone away from home or alone at home
- ❏ Crossing a bridge
- ❏ Traveling in a bus, train or car

YES   NO   9. Have you worried excessively or been anxious about several things over the past 6 months?

YES   NO   10. Are these worries present most days?

Interviewer: If NO to question 9, answer NO to question 10 and proceed to question 11.

YES   NO   11. Are these worries present most days? In the past month, were you afraid or embarrassed when others were watching you, or when you were the focus of attention? Were you afraid of being humiliated? Examples include:
- ❏ Speaking in public
- ❏ Eating in public or with others
- ❏ Writing while someone watches
- ❏ Being in social situations

YES   NO   12. In the past month, have you been bothered by thoughts, impulses, or images that you couldn't get rid of that were unwanted, distasteful, inappropriate, intrusive or distressing? Examples include:
- ❏ Were you afraid that you would act on some impulse that would be really shocking?
- ❏ Did you worry a lot about being dirty, contaminated or having germs?

❑ Did you worry a lot about contaminating others, or that you would harm someone even though you didn't want to?

❑ Did you have any fears or superstitions that you would be responsible for things going wrong?

❑ Were you obsessed with sexual thoughts, images or impulses?

❑ Did you hoard or collect lots of things?

❑ Did you have religious practice obsessions?

YES   NO   13. In the past month, did you do something repeatedly without being able to resist doing it?
Examples include:

❑ Washing or cleaning excessively

❑ Counting or checking things over and over

❑ Repeating, collecting, or arranging things

❑ Other superstitious rituals

YES   NO   14. Have you ever experienced or witnessed or had to deal with an extremely traumatic event that included actual or threatened death or serious injury to you or someone else?
Examples include:

❑ Serious accidents

❑ Sexual or physical assault

❑ Terrorist attack

❑ Being held hostage

❑ Kidnapping

❑ Fire

❑ Discovering a body

❑ Sudden death of someone close to you

❑ War

❑ Natural disaster

YES   NO   15. Have you re-experienced the awful event in a distressing way in the past month?
Examples include:

❑ Dreams

❑ Intense recollections

❑ Flashbacks

❑ Physical reactions

_____ Total number of YES responses to questions 7–15, Section B

(Continued on the next page)

SECTION C

YES   NO   16. Have you ever believed that people were spying on you, or that someone was plotting against you, or trying to hurt you?

YES   NO   17. Have you ever believed that someone was reading your mind or could hear your thoughts, or that you could actually read someone's mind or hear what another person was thinking?

YES   NO   18. Have you ever believed that someone or some force outside of yourself put thoughts in your mind that were not your own, or made you act in a way that was not your usual self? Or, have you ever felt that you were possessed?

YES   NO   19. Have you ever believed that you were being sent special messages through the TV, radio, or newspaper? Did you believe that someone you did not personally know was particularly interested in you?

YES   NO   20. Have your relatives or friends ever considered any of your beliefs strange or unusual?

YES   NO   21. Have you ever heard things other people couldn't hear, such as voices?

YES   NO   22. Have you ever had visions when you were awake or have you ever seen things other people couldn't see?

_____ Total number of YES responses to questions 16–22, Section C

SCORING THE SCREEN

YES   NO   Score indicated need for an assessment?

YES NO   If NO, did treatment team determine that an assessment was needed anyway?

SCORING THE SCREEN

Number of YES responses from Section A   _____

Number of YES responses from Section B   _____

Number of YES responses from Section C   _____

Total of YES responses from Sections A, B & C   _____

YES response to Question #4   _____

YES response to Questions # 14 and #15   _____

FIGURE 3.10A MODIFIED MINI SCREEN (MMS) SPANISH

Modified Mini Screen (MMS)

Client Name: _____ ID: _____

Interviewer: _____

Today's Date: _____ Initials (Optional) _____

SECTION A

SÍ   NO   1. ¿En las últimas dos semanas, se ha sentido deprimido/a o decaído/a la mayor parte del día, casi todos los días?

SÍ   NO   2. ¿En las últimas dos semanas, ha perdido el interés en la mayoría del las cosas o ha disfrutado menos de las cosas que usualmente le agradaban?

SÍ   NO   3. ¿En los últimos dos años, se ha sentido triste, desanimado/a o deprimido/a la mayor parte del tiempo?

SÍ   NO   4. ¿En el último mes ha pensado que estaría mejor muerto/a, o ha deseado estar muerto/a?

SÍ   NO   5. ¿Alguna vez, ha tenido un periodo de tiempo en el que se ha sentido exaltado/a, eufórico/a, o tan llena de energía, o seguro de sí mismo/a, que esto le ha ocasionado problemas u otras personas han pensado que usted no estaba en su estado habitual? (No considere períodos en el que estaba intoxicado con drogas o alcohol.)

SÍ   NO   6. ¿Ha estado usted alguna vez persistentemente irritable por varios días, de tal manera que tenía discusiones, peleaba o gritaba a personas fuera de su familia? ¿Ha usted o los demás, notado que ha estado mas irritable o que reacciona de una manera exagerada, comparada a otras personas, en situaciones que incluso usted creía justificadas?

_____ Total number of YES responses to questions 1–6, Section A

SECTION B

SÍ   NO   7. *Note: This question is in two parts. If the answer to BOTH a and b is YES, code the question YES. If the answer to either or both a and b is NO, code the question NO.*

SÍ   NO a. ¿Alguna vez o más de una vez, se sintió súbiatamente ansioso/a, asustado/a, incómodo/a o inquieto/a, incluso cuando la mayoría de la gente no sentiría de esa manera?

SÍ   NO b. ¿Estos sentimientos intensos llegan a ser aún peor dentro de 10 minutos?

SÍ   NO 8. ¿Se ha sentido particularmente incómodo/a o ansioso/a en lugares o situaciones donde podría tener un ataque de pánico, o síntomas parecidos a los que acabamos de discutir, o situaciones donde no dispondría de ayuda o escapar, pudiera resultar difícil?
Como:
❑ El estar en una multitud
❑ El permanecer en fila
❑ El estar sola fuera de casa
❑ El permanecer sola en casa
❑ El cruzar un puente
❑ El viajar en autobús, tren o automóvil

SÍ   NO 9. ¿Se ha sentido excesivamente preocupado/a o ansioso/a debido a varias cosas en los últimos 6 meses?

SÍ   NO 10. ¿Esas preocupaciones están presentes la mayoría del los días?

Interviewer: If NO to question 9, answer NO to question 10 and proceed to question 11.

SÍ   NO 11. ¿En el mes pasado, tuvo miedo o sintió vergüenza de que la estan observando, de ser el centro de atención o temió una humillación?
Incluyendo cosas como:
❑ El hablar en público
❑ Comer en público o con otros
❑ El escribir mientras alguien le mira
❑ El estar en situaciones sociales

SÍ   NO 12. ¿Este último mes, ha estado usted molesta con pensamientos recurrentes, impulsos o imágenes no deseadas, desagradables, inapropiadas, intrusas o angustiosas?
Ejemplos:
❑ La idea de estar sucia, contaminada o tener gérmenes o miedo de contaminar a otros
❑ Temor de hacerle daño a alguien sin querer

❑ Temor que actuaría en función de algún impulso

❑ Tiene temores o supersticiones de ser la responsable de que las cosas vayan mal

❑ Se obsesiona con pensamientos imágenes o impulsos sexuales

❑ Acumula o colecciona sin control

❑ Tiene obsesiones religiosas

SÍ   NO   13. ¿Durante el mes pasado, volvía hacer algo repetidamente sin poder resistir a harcerlo?

SÍ   NO   14. ¿Ha vivido o ha sido testigo de un acontecimiento extremadamente traumático, en el cual otras personas han muerto y/o otras personas o usted mismo han estado amenazadas de muerte o en su integridad física?

Ejemplos de acontecimientos traumáticos:

❑ Accidentes graves

❑ Atraco

❑ Violación

❑ Atentado terrorista

❑ Ser tomado de rehén

❑ Secuestro

❑ Incendio

❑ Descubrir un cadáver

❑ Muerte súbita de alguien cercano a usted

❑ Guerra

❑ Catástrofe natural

SÍ   NO   15. ¿Durante el mes pasado, ha revivido el evento de una manera angustiosa?

Ejemplos:

❑ Lo ha soñado

❑ Ha tenido imágenes vívidas

❑ Ha reaccionado físicamente

❑ Ha tenido memorias intensas

_____ Total number of YES responses to questions 7–15, Section B

SECTION C

SÍ   NO   16. ¿Alguna vez, ha tenido la impresión de que alguien le espiaba, o conspiraba contra usted, o que trataban de hacerle daño?

SÍ   NO   17. ¿Ha tenido usted la impresión de que alguien podía leer o escuchar sus pensamientos, o que usted podía leer o escuchar los pensamientos de otros?

SÍ   NO   18. ¿Alguna vez ha creido, que alguien o que una fuerza externa haya metido pensamientos ajenos en su mente o le hicieron actuar de una manera no usual en usted? ¿Alguna vez ha tenido la impresión de que está poseido?

SÍ   NO   19. ¿Alguna vez ha creido que le envian mensajes especiales a través de la radio, el televisor, o el periódico, o que una persona que no conocía personalmente se interesaba particularmente por usted?

SÍ   NO   20. ¿Consideran sus familiares o amigos que algunas de sus creencias son extrañas o poco usuales?

SÍ   NO   21. ¿Alguna vez, ha escuchado cosas que otras personas no podían escuchar, como voces?

SÍ   NO   22. ¿Alguna vez, estando despierto, ha tenido visiones o ha visto cosas que otros no podían ver?

_____ Total number of YES responses to questions 16–22, Section C

SCORING THE SCREEN

YES   NO   Score indicated need for an assessment?

YES   NO   If NO, did treatment team determine that an assessment was needed anyway?

SCORING THE SCREEN

Number of YES responses from Section A _____

Number of YES responses from Section B _____

Number of YES responses from Section C _____

Total of YES responses from Sections A, B & C _____

YES response to Question #4 _____

YES response to Questions # 14 and #15 _____

FIGURE 3.11. INCIDENT COMMAND SYSTEM WIRING DIAGRAM

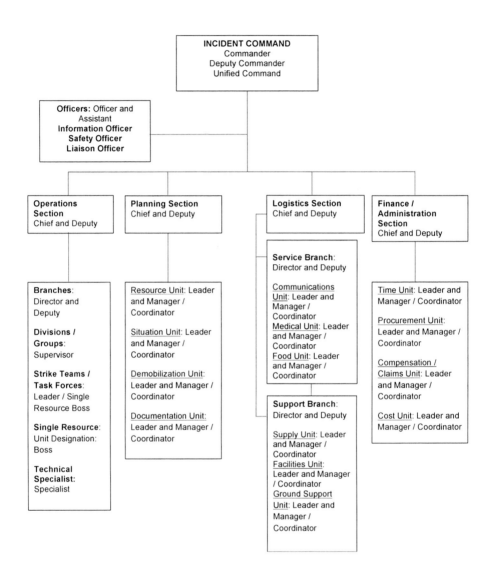

FIGURE 3.12. MILITARY HISTORY CHECKLIST

MILITARY HISTORY CHECKLIST

PATIENT DATA

Completed By: _____ Date: _____

Patient's Name: _____

Address: _____

Medical Record #: _____ Last 4 SSN: _____

VETERAN STATUS INFORMATION

YES   NO   1. Did you (or your spouse or family member)
                serve in the military?

   1a. Patient

      YES   NO   Did you serve on active duty?

      YES   NO   Did your service include combat, dangerous or
                     traumatic assignments?

      YES   NO   Do you have a copy of your DD214 discharge papers?

   1b. Did your spouse serve on active duty?
       Comments: _____

       _____

   1c. Do you have any immediate family members that served or are
       serving in the military?
       Comments: _____

MILITARY BACKGROUND

2. In which branch of the military did you serve?

   ❑ Army   ❑ Coast Guard

   ❑ Navy   ❑ Reservist or National Guard member

   ❑ Air Force   ❑ Merchant Marines during WWII

   ❑ Marines   ❑ Other _____

3. In which war era or period of service did you serve?

- ❑ WWI (4/6/17 to 11/11/18)
- ❑ WWII (12/7/41 to 12/31/46)
- ❑ Korea (6/27/50 to 1/31/55)
- ❑ Cold War
- ❑ Vietnam (8/5/64 to 5/7/75 and 2/28/61 for Veterans who served "in country" (in Vietnam) before 8/5/64)
- ❑ Gulf War (8/2/90 through a date to be set by law or presidential proclamation)
- ❑ Peace Time
- ❑ Afghanistan/Iraq (OEF/OIF)
- ❑ Other

Note: After 9/7/80, must have completed 24 months continuous active service, or the full period for which they were called or ordered to active duty.

4. Overall, how do you view your experience in the military?

_____

_____

YES NO 5. If available would you like those who care for you to have military experience?

VA BENEFITS INFORMATION

YES NO 6. Are you enrolled in VA?

YES NO 6a. Do you receive any VA benefits?

YES NO 6b. Do you have a service-connected condition?

YES NO 6c. Do you get your medications from VA?

YES NO 6d. What is the name of your VA hospital or clinic?

YES NO 6e. What is the name and contact information of your VA physician or Primary Care Provider?

YES NO 6f. Would you like to talk with someone about benefits you or your family might be eligible to receive?

3.13 The Lethality Scale of the American Academy of Crisis Interveners

Points	0	1	2	3	4	Total
Age Male (yrs)	0-12		13-44	45-64	65 and up	
Age Female (yrs)	0-12	13-44	45 and up			
Personal Resources Available	Good	Fair		Poor		
Current Stress	Low		Medium		High	
Marital Status	Married with Children	Married without Children				
Widowed or Single	Divorced					
Current Psycho-logical Function-ing	Stable			Unstable		
Other problems or symptoms	Absent			Present		
Communi-cation Channels	Open			Blocked		
Physical Condition	Good		Fair		Poor	
Suicide by Close Family Member	No		Yes			
Depressed or Agitated Currently	No				Yes	
Prior Suicidal Behavior by Subject	No		Yes			
Reactions by Signifi-cant Others to Needs of the Subject	Helpful			Not Helpful		

(Continued on the next page)

3.13 Lethality Scale *(Continued)*

Points	0	1	2	3	4	Total
Current Financial Stress	Absent		Present			
Suicidal Plan of the Subject	Has None	Plan with Few Details	Subject has Selected the Means for Suicide		Subject has a Highly Specific Plan for Suicide	
Occupation of Subject	Non-Helping Profession or Other Occupation	M.D., Dentist, Attorney, or Helping Profes-sional	Psychiatrist, Police Officer, or Unem-ployed			
Residence	Rural	Suburban	Urban			
Living Arrange-ments	Lives with Others				Lives Alone	
Time of the Year this Incident is Occurring		Spring				
Day of the Week this Incident Occurring		Sun. or Wed.	Mon.			
Recent Occurrence of Serious Arguments with Spouse or Significant Other	No	Yes				
Recently, the Subject's Significant Other Was:		The Focus of a Disap-pointment	Lost to the Subject in Some Significant Way			
						TOTAL POINTS

Source: Dr. Edward S. Rosenbluh with Permission.   *(Scoring on next page)*

Lethality Scale Scoring *(Scale on previous two pages)*

Name of Subject: _____

Date and Time Scale Completed: _____

Name of Individual Completing this Scale:_____

Criteria

Minimal Risk (0-15 points)   _____

Low Risk (16-30 points)   _____

Medium Risk (31-46 points) _____

High Risk (47-60 points)   _____

Directions for Use: Circle response in appropriate row and column. Place points from top of column in the far right column. Sum all scores under Total Points and match with total Criteria at bottom of page. Scale can be run multiple times on same subject as more information becomes available.

Comments and Action Notes:

_____

_____

_____

_____

_____

_____

_____

_____

FIGURE 5.1 – GREENSTONE'S 25, CHAPTER 5, PAGE 42

Resiliency equals:

1. Looking for benefits in encountered problems.
2. Adapting quickly to difficulties.
3. Feeling stronger in the midst of adversity.
4. Optimism. An optimistic outlook at all times.
5. Independence. Acting independently.
6. Expecting to overcome difficulties whenever and wherever met.
7. Personal durability.
8. Calmness through any storm.
9. Letting go of discouragement.
10. Staying focused.
11. Letting go of anger.
12. Intuition utilization. Trusting your feelings and your inklings.
13. Expression of feelings. Yours and others.
14. Curiousness. Creativity and seeking the truth.
15. Adaptiveness. Overcome and Prevail.
16. Willingness to learn.
17. Non-judgment of self and others.
18. Flexibility.
19. Listening well to others.
20. Anticipating problems.
21. Good self-esteem. Let the good in you always show.
22. Tolerance for ambiguity.
23. Avoidance of problems when possible.
24. Empathizing with others.
25. Self-confidence.

FIGURE 5.2 HEAT RELATED ILLNESSES AND PREVENTION TIPS

HEAT CRAMPS	HEAT EXHAUSTION	HEAT STROKE
Painful muscle spasms following activity	Heavy Sweating	Lack of sweating usually
Skin usually moist and cool	Paleness	Reddish tinge to skin
Pulse normal or slightly raised	Cold and clammy skin	Body temperature 103° F or higher
Body temperature essentially normal	Muscle cramps	Strong rapid pulse
	Irritability	Confusion or unconsciousness
	Tiredness or weakness	Possible delirium or coma
	Dizziness or headache	Throbbing headache or dizziness
	"Sick Stomach" or vomiting	"Sick Stomach" or nausea

Prevention

1. Drink plenty of fluids that are non-alcoholic regardless of your activity level.

2. Do not drink fluids that contain caffeine, alcohol, or large amounts of sugar. These cause loss of even greater amounts of body fluid.

3. Wear lightweight, light colored and loose fitting clothing.

4. Stay indoors and in an air conditioned place if possible.

5. Take cool showers or baths with frequent sponging with cool or cold washcloths or move to an air conditioned place. Electric fans may provide comfort but when temperature is in the high 90's, fans will not prevent heat related illnesses.

6. Never leave anyone in a closed and parked vehicle.

7. Schedule vigorous activities and sports for cooler times of the day.

8. Check regularly on people at greater risk of hyperthermia including infants, young children, people aged 65 and older, people who have a mental illness, and those who are physically ill. Check especially on those with heart disease or high blood pressure.

FIGURE 5.3 HAND CLEANSING

- Hand cleansing removes germs that may be picked up at any time that hands touch persons or contaminated items.

- Cleansing can be done with soap and water.

- Cleansing can be done with waterless hand cleansers.

- Hand washing and cleansing is the single most important process to prevent the spread of microorganisms or germs that can cause infection.

- Cleansing with soap and water requires briskly rubbing all surfaces of the hands, including the wrists, to work up a lather.

- This is followed by rinsing the hands under running water.

- This process removes visible soil, blood or fluids as well as many germs.

- Hand cleansing with soap containing an antimicrobial agent kills most germs.

- Cleaning hands with waterless alcohol-based hand liquids requires briskly rubbing all hand surfaces, including wrists, until all hands are dry.

- This process rapidly kills most germs on contact.

- Soap that contains an antimicrobial agent such as, but not limited to, chlorhexidine, works well.

- Both you and victims or sufferers with whom you may be in contact should take these cleansing precautions.

- Hand cleansing should be done before contact with others or with items.

- Hand cleansing should be done after contact with others or with items.

- The importance of hand cleansing should not be underestimated for both field and non-field environments.

FIGURE 7.1 EMERGENCY SUPPORT FUNCTIONS, CHAPTER 7, PAGE 61

Emergency Support Functions

Emergency Support Functions (ESFs) is the grouping of governmental and certain private sector capabilities into an organizational structure to provide support, resources, program implementation, and services that are most likely needed to save lives, protect property and the environment, restore essential services and critical infrastructure, and help victims and communities return to normal following domestic incidents.

Emergency Support Functions

- ESF1   Transportation
- ESF2   Communications
- ESF3   Public Works and Engineering
- ESF4   Firefighting
- ESF5   Emergency Management
- ESF6   Mass Care, Housing, and Human Services
- ESF7   Resources Support
- ESF8   Public Health and Medical Services
- ESF9   Urban Search and Rescue
- ESF10 Oil and Hazardous Materials Response
- ESF11 Agriculture and Natural Resources
- ESF12 Energy
- ESF13 Public Safety and Security
- ESF14 Long-term Community Recovery and Mitigation
- ESF15 External Affairs

There are 15 ESFs, and Health and Human Services (HHS) is the primary agency responsible for Emergency Support Functions (ESF) 8 – Public Health and Medical Services. ESF 8 is coordinated by the Secretary of HHS principally through the Assistant Secretary for Preparedness and Response (ASPR). ESF 8 resources can be activated through the Stafford Act or the Public Health Service Act.

ESF 8 – Public Health and Medical Services

ESF 8 – Public Health and Medical Services provides the mechanism for coordinated Federal assistance to supplement State, Tribal, and local resources in response to the following:

- Public health and medical care needs
- Veterinary and/or animal health issues in coordination with the U.S. Department of Agriculture (USDA)
- Potential or actual incidents of national significance
- A developing potential health and medical situation

Emergency Support Functions *(Continued)*

ESF 8 involves supplemental assistance to state, tribal, and jurisdictional governments in identifying and meeting the public health and medical needs of victims of major disasters or public health and medical emergencies. This support is categorized in the following functional areas:

- Assessment of public health/medical needs
- Public health surveillance
- Medical care personnel
- Medical equipment and supplies
- Patient movement
- Hospital care
- Outpatient services
- Victim decontamination
- Safety and security of human drugs, biologics, medical devices, veterinary drugs, etc.
- Blood products and services
- Food safety and security
- Agriculture feed safety and security
- Worker health and safety
- All hazard consultation and technical assistance and support
- Mental health and substance abuse care
- Public health and medical information
- Vector control
- Potable water/wastewater and solid waste disposal, and other environmental health issues
- Victim identification/mortuary services
- Veterinary services.
- Federal public health and medical assistance consists of medical materiel, personnel, and technical assistance.

Health and Medical Response Lead Partners

HHS leads and coordinates the overall health and medical response to national-level incidents through coordination, along with the following:

- Department of Agriculture
- Department of Transportation

Emergency Support Functions *(Continued)*

- Department of Defense
- Department of Veterans Affairs
- Department of State
- Agency for International Development
- Department of Energy
- Environmental Protection Agency
- Department of Homeland Security
- General Services Administration
- Department of Interior
- U.S. Postal Service
- Department of Justice
- American Red Cross
- Department of Labor

Assistant Secretary for Preparedness and Response (ASPR), 200 Independence Ave., SW, Washington, DC 20201.

U.S. Department of Health and Human Services

The Recovery Support Function Coordinating Agency, with the assistance of the Federal Emergency Management Agency, provides leadership, coordination and oversight for that particular. When coordinating agencies are activatedto lead a Recovery Support Function, primary agencies and supporting organizations are expected to be responsive to the function related communication and coordination needs.

Health and Social Services

Coordinating Agency:
Department of Health and Human Services

Primary Agencies:
Corporation for National and Community Service, Department of Homeland Security *(Federal Emergency Management Agency/National Preparedness and Protection Directive and Civil Rights and Civil Liberties)*

Department of Interior

Department of Justice

Department of Labor

Education Department and Veterans Affairs

Health and Social Services *(Continued)*

Supporting Organizations:

Department of Transportation

Small Business Administration

Department of Treasury

Department of Agriculture

Veterans Affairs

American Red Cross

National Organizations Active in Disasters

Mission

The Health and Social Services Recovery Support Function mission is for the Federal Government to assist locally-led recovery efforts in the restoration of the public health, health care and social services networks to promote the resilience, health and well-being of affected individuals and communities.

FIGURE 7.2 – THE NATIONAL DISASTER RECOVERY SUPPORT FUNCTIONS
CHAPTER 7, PAGE 64

The National Disaster Recovery Framework introduces six new Recovery Support Functions that are led by designated federal coordinating agencies at the national level.

Recovery Support Functions involve partners in the local, state and tribal governments and private and nonprofit sectors not typically involved in emergency support functions but critically needed in disaster recovery. These new partners may include public and private organizations that have experience with permanent housing financing, economic development, advocacy for underserved populations and long-term community planning. The processes used for facilitating recovery are more flexible, context based and collaborative in approach than the task-oriented approach used during the response phase of an incident.

Recovery processes should be scalable and based on demonstrated recovery needs.Each Recovery Support Function has a designated coordinating agency along with primary agencies and supporting organizations with programs relevant to the functional area.

FIGURE 7.3 – NATIONAL DISASTER RECOVERY FRAMEWORK,
CHAPTER 7, PAGE 65

National Disaster Recovery Framework

Function

The core recovery capability for health and social services is the ability to restore and improve health and social services networks to promote the resilience, health, independence and well being of the whole community. The Health and Social Services RSF outlines the Federal framework to support locally-led recovery efforts to address public health, health care facilities and coalitions, and essential social services needs. For the purposes of this RSF, the use of the term health will refer to and include public health, behavioral health and medical services.

This Annex establishes (1) a Federal focal point for coordinating Federal recovery efforts specifically for health and social services needs; and, (2) a Federal operational framework outlining how Federal agencies plan to support local health and social services recovery efforts. This framework is flexible and can adjust during a disaster to complement local efforts, as needed.

Pre-Disaster: The Health and Social Services Recovery Support Function

- Incorporates planning for the transition from response to recovery into preparedness and operational plans, in close collaboration with ESFs #3, #6, #8 and #11.
- Incorporates planning for the transition from post-incident recovery operations back to a steady-state into preparedness and operational plans.
- Develops strategies to address recovery issues for health, behavioral health and social services – particularly the needs of response and recovery workers, children, seniors, people living with disabilities, people with functional needs, people from diverse cultural origins, people with limited English proficiency and underserved populations.
- Promotes the principles of sustainability, resilience and mitigation into preparedness and operational plans.

Post-Disaster: The Health and Social Services Recovery Support Function

- Maintains situational awareness to identify and mitigate potential recovery obstacles during the response phase.

- Leverages response, emergency protection measures and hazard mitigation resources during the response phase to expedite recovery.

- Provides technical assistance in the form of impact analyses and supports recovery planning of public health, health care and human services infrastructure.

- Conducts Federal Health and Social Services Recovery Support Function assessments with primary agencies.

- Identifies and coordinates Federal Health and Social Services specific missions with primary agencies

- When activated by the Federal Disaster Recovery Coordinator, the primary and supporting departments and agencies deploy in support of the Health and Social Services Recovery Support Function mission, as appropriate.

- Establishes communication and information-sharing forum(s) for Health and Social Services RSF stakeholders with the State and/or community.

- Coordinates and leverages applicable Federal resources for health and social services.

- Develops and implements a plan to transition from Federal Health and Social Services recovery operations back to a steady-state.

- Identifies and coordinates with other local, State, Tribal and Federal partners to assess food, animal, water and air conditions to ensure safety.

- Evaluates the effectiveness of Federal Health and Social Services recovery efforts.

- Provides technical assistance in the form of impact analyses and recovery planning support of public health, health care, and human services infrastructure.

- Identifies and coordinates with other local, State, Tribal and Federal partners the assessment of food, animal, water and air conditions to ensure their safety.

Outcomes for the Health and Social Services Recovery Support Function

- Restore the capacity and resilience of essential health and social services to meet ongoing and emerging post-disaster community needs.

- Encourage behavioral health systems to meet the behavioral health needs of affected individuals, response and recovery workers, and the community.

- Promote self-sufficiency and continuity of the health and well-being of affected individuals; particularly the needs of children, seniors, people living with disabilities whose members may have additional functional needs, people from diverse origins, people with limited English proficiency, and underserved populations.

- Assist in the continuity of essential health and social services, including schools.

- Reconnect displaced populations with essential health and social services.

- Protect the health of the population and response and recovery workers from the longer-term effects of a post-disaster environment.

- Promote clear communications and public health messaging to provide accurate, appropriate and accessible information; ensure information is developed and disseminated in multiple mediums, multi-lingual formats, alternative formats, is age-appropriate and user-friendly and is accessible to underserved populations.

September 2011

FIGURE 8.1, CHAPTER 8, PAGE 72
FIELD PERSONAL EQUIPMENT CHECK LIST
THE 2-3-4 RULE (2010)

The 2-3-4 Rule

2 bags
   One personal small bag to be carried
      (Ready Bag)

   One large bag to be shipped or palletized
      (Main Flight Bag)

3 days of food, one MRE meal

4 quarts of water with one quart in Ready Bag

FIGURE 8.2 – WHAT TO BRING, PAGE 72

What to Bring

The following list is to use when preparing for deployment. This list is devised so that all deployed team members are self-sufficient and able to care for themselves.

- Two bags are to be utilized. First, a large MAIN BAG for shipping or for palletization which will probably not be available in transit or for up to several days. This bag needs to be rugged and smart in design with a capacity of 4500 cubic inches or better.
- The second bag is a smaller READY BAG to carry items needed in flight. The Ready Bag is your carry-on with personal items. Remember your Ready Bag must meet commercial air carriers requirements for overhead bins if flying. Most folks use a backpack.
- Make sure your name is on both bags.
- The Main Flight bags must weigh less than 50 pounds if flying commercial.

FIGURE 8.3, CHAPTER 8, PAGE 73 – MAIN FLIGHT BAG

Use the following list as a guide. It will take a deployment or two before you know what to carry.

MAIN FLIGHT BAG "72 hour Pack"

CLOTHING

Long durable trousers . . . . 1–6 pair

Long sleeve durable shirt . . . . 1–2 each

Durable shorts . . . . 1–2 pair

Distinguishing "T" shirts . . . . 2–4 each

Distinguishing polo shirts . . . . 1–6 each

Boots black . . . . 1 pair

Tennis shoes . . . . 1 pair

Shower shoes . . . . 1 pair

Bandana . . . . 1–2 each

Underwear . . . . 3–6 plus

Socks . . . . 3–6 plus

Swimwear 1

Camp clothes . . . . as needed

COLD WEATHER – ADDITIONAL CLOTHING

Long johns – polypro's . . . . 2–3 each

Wool sweater . . . . 1 each

Down Jackets/Coats . . . . 1 each
   (polar guard)

Gloves or Mittens . . . . 1–2 pair

Wool socks . . . . 1–2 pair

Cold weather boots . . . . 1 pair

COOKING AND FOOD

Knife, spoon and fork set

36 hours of rations/MREs

Cup

High energy snacks

MAIN FLIGHT BAG "72 hour Pack" (Continued)

SLEEPING

Sleeping bag (+15 degrees)

Foam pad

Ground cloth

Pillow – inflatable

MISCELLANEOUS

Head lamp (2nd light source)

Extra batteries/bulbs

Matches in waterproof container

Face mask/Dust mask

Goggles/safety glasses

Tape, safety pens, sewing kit

Towels, wash cloth

Hand mirror

550/P cord 50'

Large trash bags

Nail clippers, etc.

FIGURE 8.4, CHAPTER 8, PAGE 74 – READY BAG "24 HOUR PACK"

READY BAG "24 hour Pack"

Must have with you:

Organizational ID and Driver's License

Money and Credit Cards

Passport or Birth Certificate (out of country)

Emergency Phone Numbers

CLOTHING

HAT – Ball cap/Boonie . . . . 1 each

Rain Gear . . . . 1 set

Bandana . . . . 1 each

BDU – Consider carrying one pair of BDU pants and T–shirt in a zip lock bag.

Socks and underwear in zip lock bag.

PERSONAL PROTECTION

Eye protection . . . . 1 set

Ear plugs . . . . 1–2 sets

Leather work gloves . . . . 1–2 sets

Flash light/s with spare batteries . . . . . 1–2 each

Personal first aid kit . . . . 1 each

PERSONAL GEAR

Razor/blades	Shaving Cream
Toothbrush/paste	Sunscreen
Comb/brush	Deodorant
Shampoo	Bar soap
Hand lotion	Hand wipes
Facial tissue	Toilet tissue
Eye wash (Visine)	Lip balm
Insect repellant	Dog tags
Medication (14 day supply)	Glasses and sun glasses
Foot Care (moleskin, powder)	Detergent (clothing)

READY BAG "24 hour Pack" *(Continued)*

MEDICAL EQUIPMENT
(as required and authorized by your training and specialty)

Stethoscope . . . . 1 each

Trauma Shears . . . . 1 pair

Bandage Shears . . . . 1 pair

Pen Light . . . . 1 each

Pens . . . . 5-6 each

Note Pads . . . . 1-2 each

Gloves . . . . Several

PERSONAL FIRST-AID KIT
Every member should carry a personal first-aid kit in the left cargo pocket of their BDUs. Your items will fit nicely in a small zip lock bag and should include:

Band-Aids . . . . 12 each

2" x 2" or 3" x 3" gauze . . . . 6 each

Betadine pads . . . . 6 each

Moleskin . . . . 1 each

Small roll of gauze . . . . 1 each

Triangular bandage . . . . 1-2 each

Antibiotic ointment . . . . 4 each

FIGURE 8.5, CHAPTER 8, PAGE 76 – PROHIBITED ITEMS

PROHIBITED ITEMS

Do not carry the following: *(Please check with TSA before flying)*

Explosives	Compressed gas
Radioactive material	Guns
Ammunition	Corrosives
Poison	Infectious substance
Magnetized material	Oxidizers
Flammable liquid or solid	Knives
Aerial flares	Smoke signals
Mace	Pepper spray
Propane/Stove fuel	Aerosols
CO2 cartridges	Thermometers (mercury)
Lighter fluid	Wet batteries
Smoke detectors	Expensive jewelry
Perishable foods	Curling irons/Hot rollers
Alcoholic Beverages	Drugs (illegal)

Interpreter Check List

☐ 1.   Interpreters must be chosen carefully prior to actual healthcare involvement.

☐ 2.   Interpreters should be recruited from reputable agencies that provide such services and have interpreters readily available and properly trained according to these guidelines.

☐ 3.   In the alternative to an agency, a specific person with the required skills should be sought, evaluated, and trained by the healthcare or behavioral health team.

☐ 4.   The interpreter only acts as a "word machine" for the primary provider.

☐ 5.   The interpreter does not conduct the ongoing dialogue with, or examination of, the patient, victim or examinee.

☐ 6.   Interpreters must say to the person exactly what the healthcare provider says and in the same way as the provider says it; word for word.

☐ 7.   Similarly, the interpreter must say to the primary behavioral healthcare or crisis intervention provider exactly what the patient says and in the same way that the patient says it. No deviations are permitted.

☐ 8.   Interpreters should not paraphrase what either the healthcare provider or the sufferer says.

☐ 9.   Information about the patient's tone, inflection, cultural meanings, etc., will be given directly to the behavioral healthcare provider if such nuances may not successfully cross cultural boundaries. The interpreter should be instructed to do this by the primary healthcare provider.

☐ 10. Interpreters should not add personal interpretations about what the patient or healthcare provider is saying.

☐ 11. Healthcare providers must confirm that the interpreter should be fluent specifically in English and in the language of the non–English-speaking person.

☐ 12. The interpreter should have no conflicts of interest.

☐ 13. When using the interpreter, the primary healthcare provider should speak in short phrases in order to allow for accurate translations. (Chunking)

☐ 14. The behavioral healthcare provider should always speak directly to the patient or victim and maintain eye contact: do not look at the interpreter.

☐ 15. The interpreter should translate in short phrases utilizing the concept of "chunking."

☐ 16. The interpreter is not part of the behavioral healthcare team unless specifically needed in that capacity.

☐ 17. Remember, the interpreter only translates. Nothing more.

☐ 18. For telephone translations, a secondary phone line attached to the primary phone will be needed so that the interpreter can hear both sides of the conversation.

☐ 19. Interpreters should not be used in situations within which they may feel uncomfortable or threatened.

☐ 20. If you have concerns regarding the accuracy of an interpreter or of a translation, have the interaction verified by another person fluent in both languages, or by another bona fide, appropriately trained, interpreter.

☐ 21. The behavioral healthcare provider should confirm the victim's ability to speak English. If the patient or victim speaks at least some English, communicate directly in English, and have the interpreter stand-by to assist if needed.

☐ 22. Speaking with someone who only speaks some or minimal English will tend to slow down the conversation and examination.

☐ 23. Interpreters must convey to the behavioral healthcare provider idiomatic nuances in the verbal exchanges that may not be obvious to the listener. This should be done directly to the provider or intervener.

☐ 24. The interpreter should not insert his or her own beliefs or possible alternative approaches to the victim's problems or difficulties.

☐ 25. The interpreter should not editorialize or express personal opinions or emotions except as requested by the behavioral healthcare provider; never to the patient or victim. (DiVasto, 1996).

☐ 26. It is good practice for the interpreter to have a small note pad and pen or pencil available to them throughout the interaction.

☐ 27. The interpreter should use the small notepad only to capture those items spoken by either the behavioral health provider or the patient that may be too long in content for the interpreter to remember.

☐ 28. As seen in Figure 11.1, the arrangement of interpreter, provider and patient or victim may be set differently depending on the circumstances that exist at the time.

☐ 29. Interpreters should interpret exclamations from the patient or provider in the way that they are presented. EG. If the patient or victim exclaims, "Ouch" in their language, the interpreter should repeat the exclamation in English with the same emotional level used by the patient.

☐ 30. An experienced interpreter may be able to do ongoing interpretation as either the provider or victim/patient is talking.

FIGURE 11.1, CHAPTER 11, PAGE 90 – INTERPRETER, PROVIDER,
NON-ENGLISH SPEAKER ARRANGEMENT

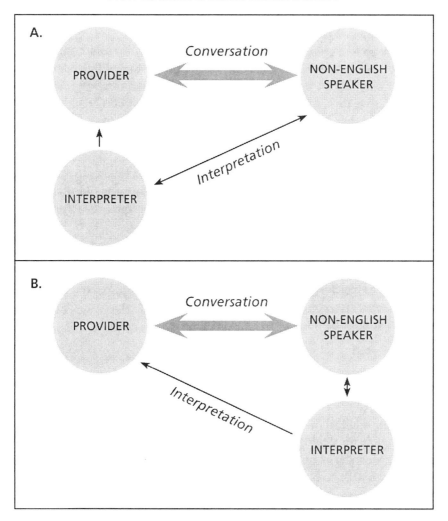

Advance Directive to Family Members of a First Responder Deployed in Crisis or Disaster Venues

When we go to a crisis as a first responder, we need to remind our families and / or loved ones of the myriad of things that will need to be done for us while we are away. Not at all the same as a medical advanced care directive, this is a list of things, particular to a certain crisis event, that we need the troops at home to handle. Whether we are a first responder, civilian or military, psychologist, fire fighter, EMT, or other professional we need to tell those at home what we want to happen while we are deployed or should we be seriously injured or subject to other unexpected forces that might get in the way of performing our duties on the home front. The recipient and acceptor agree and is charged to perform as requested.

Things that appear on this list can be as mundane as paying the mortgage and making sure someone goes to Billy's Little League Game or as vital as checking on an elderly relative. In general, the requests will stay the same from one deployment to the next. Reasons to change your directive might include:

1. The start of a new decade of your life.
2. Known risks from a specific deployment.
3. The death or incapacitation of a loved one.
4. Divorce or other family realignment.
5. Your medical or psychological status changes but you are still eligible for deployment.
6. New concerns or directives that you have neglected to include previously.

Be aware: If you execute a new directive, the old version should be returned and destroyed to avoid confusion. Remember that this directive does not supplant the need for an Advance Directive for Healthcare, a Durable Power of Attorney for Healthcare, or any other Power of Attorney or relevant legal documents. For these, as well as for all legal documents, consult a competent attorney.

Other reminders:
1. Check to be sure that the directives listed above will be in force in any state where you might receive healthcare.
2. Be sure you have read carefully all the instructions for completing the forms and where relevant they have been reviewed by your physician.

3. Photocopy or print a second set of the form before you begin to fill it out in case you need a "do-over".

4. Talk with your family, friends, and physicians about your advance care directives. Make sure that those responsible for carrying out your wishes understand them and are willing to honor your choices.

5. Photocopy the signed form and give one to everyone concerned, including your children. Even if your children are not asked to perform any duties they need to know what you have instructed others to do to avoid any surprises should you not return as expected.

6. Leave copies of the pertinent materials online in your personal health records, with your physician, hospital and any others who have a role in your planning.

Advance Directive to Family Members of a First Responder Deployed in Crisis or Disaster Venues[1]

Instructions: Fill out the pertinent information in the space provided, have those involved sign and date the form, make the number of copies needed to provide one each for all concerned. Notify other friends/loved ones/children of the existence of the form and what is included.

Directive issued by:

Print your name_____

Signature _____ Date Signed _____

Effective date or deployment covered by this document _____

Issued To:

Spouse _____ Date Signed _____

Partner _____ Date Signed _____

Child _____ Date Signed _____

Child _____ Date Signed _____

Child _____ Date Signed _____

Child _____ Date Signed _____

Other (Specify Relationship) _____ Date Signed _____

Specific directives, instructions and relevant performance dates
(if applicable). For example: Pay mortgage first of each month.

1. _____
2. _____
3. _____
4. _____
5. _____
6. _____
7. _____
8. _____
9. _____
10. _____

Other instructions: _____

_____

_____

_____

_____

Appendix B
Supplemental Reading

How to Protect Yourself from Arthropods and Others

Overview

Poor sanitation and improper waste disposal under wartime conditions greatly increase the disease vector potential of such common pests as filth flies and rodents. Even in mobile field situations these "camp followers" have historically amplified sanitation problems, often resulting in epidemics of diarrheal diseases that have caused many casualties. The threat is even greater in urban areas converted to temporary or semipermanent military use. A dangerous temptation in field training or in deployment operations is to ignore the field sanitation standards. Some people think, "The rules don't apply here." Yielding to that temptation can cost your health and the health of those around you. There is no excuse for forgetting to bring protective equipment or failing to use it. Be sure to follow all safety precautions on all labels of the pesticides that you use. They are there for a reason – to protect your health.

Use the Department of Defense insect / arthropod repellents

The concurrent use of a skin insect repellent (N, N-diethyl-M-toluamide [DEET], NSN 6840-01-284-3982) and a clothing insect repellent (permethrin [NSN 6840-01-278-1336 and 6840-01-345-0237]) is necessary to obtain maximum protection against insects / arthropods.

Apply N, N-DIETHYL-M-TOLUAMIDE

- Apply DEET insect repellent to all exposed skin.
- Follow label directions.
- Apply a light, even coating to exposed skin, not under clothing.
- DO NOT apply to the eyes and lips, or to damaged skin.
- One application may last 8 to 12 hours; if you receive bites, reapply a light uniform coating of repellent.
- Application of DEET can be safely used with camouflage face paint. Apply a thin layer of DEET first, then apply face paint.

Note: Reapplication of DEET may be necessary (check container label) due to heavy sweating, or after river-crossing operations, exposure to rain, or in locations where arthropod density is very high.

Apply Permethrin clothing repellents
to field uniforms / sleeping equipment

- Permethrin is the most effective clothing repellent available.
- Treat military field uniforms, including Nomex?/Kevlar uniforms, tent liners, ground cloths, and bed nets with permethrin. This should be done before wearing in field training or military operations. Follow label instructions when applying to clothing.
- Permethrin will remain in the material after repeated washings.
- Treated uniforms can be safely worn in the rain or when crossing rivers or streams.

Note: Permethrin does not rinse out in cold water (or rain or streams).

- DO NOT apply directly to skin, to underwear, or to cap.
- DO NOT wear treated uniforms unless they are first thoroughly dried after treating.
- Apply permethrin outdoors or in well-ventilated areas only.
- Wear uniform as your commander directs.
- Wear a loose fitting uniform, not tightly tailored, to prevent arthropods from biting through the fabric; repair tears / holes.
- When the arthropod threat is high:
    Blouse pants in boots and completely lace boots.
    Tuck undershirt in at waist.
    Wear sleeves down.
    Button blouse / shirt at the neck and wrist.
- Do not use aftershave lotion, cologne, or perfumed deodorants or soaps in the field; they attract arthropods.
- Wear headgear (cap, helmet, arthropod head net) when necessary to protect your head.

Keep your body and uniform clean

- Bathe every day if possible, or at least once a week. Good personal hygiene practices reduce infestation of insects such as body lice and mites.
- Wash your uniform frequently (a minimum of every 7 days) to remove arthropods and their eggs which may be attached to the uniform. If the situation permits, use the quartermaster laundry; otherwise, use a stream, lake, or washbasin. Air-dry uniforms, especially underwear and socks, if possible.

Follow medical advice

- Take medications that help prevent diseases (such as anti-malaria pills) when directed by your commander.
- Use medications, such as cream / shampoo, when prescribed by medical personnel for treatment of lice, chiggers, poison ivy, and so forth.

Protect yourself at night

- Ensure your bed net is in good repair.
- Use your bed net when sleeping.
- Tuck net under sleeping pad or sleeping bag so there are no openings.
- Follow the label directions and precautions when using DOD-approved insect spray (for example, Insecticide, Aerosol d-PHENOTHRIN, 2%) if insects are present inside the bed net (and inside closed tent). Allow vapors to disperse for 10 minutes before entering the enclosure.
- Treat bed net with permethrin for added protection.
- Repair holes in your bed net. Generously apply DEET skin repellent to those areas likely to touch the insect net during sleep (knees, hands, elbows, and feet) to prevent bites through holes in the fabric.

Protect yourself from other medically important arthropods and animals

Spiders, Scorpions, and Centipedes

- Remove spiders from tents or buildings.
- Shake out and inspect clothing, shoes, and bedding before use.
- Eliminate collections of papers, unused boxes, scrap lumber, and metal.
- Thoroughly clean beneath and behind large items; spiders and scorpions may be resting in these areas.
- Check field latrines before use; run a small stick under the rim of the latrine hole to dislodge any spiders or scorpions there. Spiders and scorpions may rest under toilet seat or inside latrine box.
- Wear gloves when handling paper, cloth, lumber, or other items that have been stored for long periods.
- Check around rocks and logs before resting against them.
- Use a long-handled tool or stick to turn over debris before removing it.

- Remove accumulations of boards, rocks, and other debris to eliminate the resting / hiding areas of spiders and scorpions.
- Wear leather gloves to remove rocks, lumber, and such from the ground.

Note: In many locations worldwide, centipedes are more of a problem than scorpions, but the PPM (Personal Protection Measures) are the same for both pests.

Snakes

- Do not handle, play with, or disturb snakes or other wildlife.
- Avoid swimming in areas where snakes abound.
- Keep hands off rock ledges where snakes may be hiding or sunning.
- Look over the area before sitting down, especially if in deep grass or among rocks.
- If snakes are known to inhabit the area, sleep off the ground, if possible.
- If military situation permits, avoid walking about an area during the period from dusk to complete daylight, as many snakes are active during this period.
- Avoid camping near piles of brush, rocks, or other debris.
- Never step over large rocks or logs without first checking to see what is on the other side.
- Turn rocks and logs toward you when they have to be removed so you will be shielded should snakes be beneath them.
- Handle freshly killed snakes only with a long-handled tool or stick; snakes can inflict fatal bites by reflex action after their death.

Note: If bitten, try to kill the snake and bring its head with you to the medical treatment facility. If you cannot bring the snake's head with you, get an accurate description of the snake to assist medical personnel in treating you. DO NOT PANIC!

Domestic and wild animals or birds

- Do not handle or approach so-called "pets."
- Exclude such animals from your work and living areas, unless cleared by veterinary personnel.
- Do not collect or support (feed or shelter) stray or domestic animals / birds in the unit area, unless cleared by veterinary personnel.

Retrieved from www.armystudyguide.com, April 6, 2015.

A Quick Guide to Napping

Napping Quick Guide (The Greenstone list)

1. Nap as often as you can responsibly.

2. Best nap times are between 1:00 pm and 4:00 pm.

3. Drink a cup of caffeinated coffee just prior to your nap. You will sleep better and when you awake, the caffeine will kick in and you will feel refreshed.

4. Naps should be at least 20 minutes long; no longer than 60 minutes. REM sleep will not occur during this time so deep sleep will not result.

5. Take your naps sitting up in a chair or stretched out somewhere comfortable.

The Expert's Guide to Napping

A short snooze during the day will boost your mood and your intelligence – but there's more to it than simply closing your eyes.

The key to the perfect nap

Find a safe, quiet, comfortable place, preferably one where you can lie down. (It takes about 50% longer to fall asleep sitting upright.)

Calm your body by breathing slowly and deeply. Concentrate on relaxing your muscles one group at a time.

If noise is an issue, put in earplugs or turn on some white noise.

Set an alarm.

Darken the room or use eyeshades.

Have a light blanket handy in case you get chilly, but nothing too heavy. (Excess warmth can make you oversleep.)

Quiet your mind by repeating a mantra, taking a mental walk at a relaxing place like a beach, or counting sheep or floating zeds.

From: *The Guardian*, Monday 26 January 2009

For years, napping has been derided as a sign of laziness. We are "caught" napping or "found asleep at the switch". But lately napping has garnered new respect, thanks to scientific evidence that midday dozing benefits both mental acuity and overall health. A slew of recent studies have shown that naps boost alertness, creativity, mood, and productivity in the later hours of the day.

A nap of 60 minutes improves alertness for up to 10 hours. Research on pilots shows that a 26-minute "NASA" nap in flight (while the plane is manned by a copilot) enhanced performance by 34% and overall alertness by 54%. One Harvard study published last year showed that a 45-minute nap improves learning and memory. Napping reduces stress and lowers the risk of heart attack and stroke, diabetes, and excessive weight gain.

Getting even the briefest nap is better than nothing. A 2008 study in Düsseldorf showed that the onset of sleep may trigger active memory processes that remain effective even if sleep is limited to only a few minutes. And last year, a British study suggested that just knowing a nap was coming was enough to lower blood pressure.

Naps make you brainier, healthier, safer. But to understand how you can nap best, you need to understand your body.

For how long should you rest?
In designing the optimal nap you need to grasp its potential components. During sleep, your brain's electrical activity goes through a five-phase cycle.

A short afternoon catnap of 20 minutes yields mostly Stage 2 sleep, which enhances alertness and concentration, elevates mood, and sharpens motor skills. To boost alertness on waking, you can drink a cup of coffee before you nap. Caffeine requires 20 or 30 minutes to take effect, so it will kick in just as you're waking. Naps of up to 45 minutes may also include rapid eye movement (REM) sleep, which enhances creative thinking and boosts sensory processing.

Limit your nap to 45 minutes or less, if you need to spring into action after dozing. Otherwise, you may drift into slow-wave sleep. Waking from this stage results in sleep inertia, that grogginess and disorientation that can last for half an hour or more.

You might want to take a long nap, at least 90 minutes. Many of us get about an hour to an hour-and-a-half less sleep per night than we need.

One recent study shows that the sleep-deprived brain toggles between normal activity and complete lapses, or failures, a dangerous state of slowed responses and foggy inattention. Sound familiar?

Naps of 90 to 120 minutes usually comprise all stages, including REM and deep slow-wave sleep, which helps to clear your mind, improve memory recall, and recoup lost sleep. Longer naps in the morning yield more REM sleep, while those in the afternoon offer more slow-wave sleep. A nap that is long enough to include a full sleep cycle, at least 90 minutes, will limit sleep inertia by allowing you to wake from REM sleep.

The science of sleep

Why do we need to nap?
Most mammals sleep for short periods throughout the day. Humans have consolidated sleep into one long period, but our bodies are programmed for two periods of intense sleepiness: in the early morning, from about 2 a.m. to 4 a.m., and in the afternoon, between 1 p.m. and 3 p.m. This midday wave of drowsiness is not due to heat or a heavy lunch (it occurs even if we skip eating) but from an afternoon quiescent (not active) phase in our physiology, which diminishes our reaction time, memory, coordination, mood, and alertness.

Are you a lark or an owl?
To determine the best time to nap, it helps to know your "chronotype". What time would you get up and go to sleep if you were entirely free to plan your day? If you're a lark, apt to wake as early as 6 a.m. and go to sleep around 9 p.m. or 10 p.m., you're going to feel your nap need around 1 p.m. or 1:30 p.m.

If you're an owl, preferring to go to bed after midnight or 1 a.m., and to wake around 8 a.m. or 9 a.m., your afternoon "sleep gate" will open later, closer to 2:30 p.m. or 3 p.m.

5 Reasons Why You Should Take a Nap Every Day

It is suggested that you seriously consider taking a daily nap for the following five reasons:

1. **A nap restores alertness.** The National Sleep Foundation recommends a short nap of 20–30 minutes "for improved alertness and performance without leaving you feeling groggy or interfering with nighttime sleep."

2. **A nap prevents burnout.** In our always-on culture, we go, go, go. However, we were not meant to race without rest. Doing so leads to stress, frustration, and burnout. Taking a nap is like a system reboot. It relieves stress and gives you a fresh start.

3. **A nap heightens sensory perception.** According to Dr. Sandra C. Mednick, author of *Take a Nap, Change Your Life*, napping can restore the sensitivity of sight, hearing, and taste. Napping also improves your creativity by relaxing your mind and allowing new associations to form in it.

4. **A nap reduces the risk of heart disease.** Did you know those who take a midday siesta at least three times a week are 37 percent less likely to die of heart disease? Working men are 64 percent less likely! It's true, according to a 2007 study published in the *Archives of Internal Medicine*. Dimitrios Trichopoulos, of the Harvard School of Public Health in Boston, who led the study said, "Taking a nap could turn out to be an important weapon in the fight against coronary mortality."

5. **A nap makes you more productive.** Numerous medical studies have shown workers becoming increasingly unproductive as the day wears on. But a 2002 Harvard University study demonstrated a 30-minute nap boosted the performance of workers, returning their productivity to beginning-of-the-day levels.

Napping Tips

Here are a few practices that have been found to helpful.

1. **Be consistent.** Try to nap at the same time every day. This helps stabilize your circadian rhythms and maximize the benefits.

2. **Keep it short.** Avoid "sleep inertia," that feeling of grogginess and disorientation that can come from awakening from a deep sleep. Long naps can also negatively impact nighttime sleep. 20–30 minutes are best. Set an alarm on your phone to avoid oversleeping.

3. **Turn off the lights.** Light acts as a cue for our bodies. Darkness communicates it is time to shut down—or go into standby mode. If you can't turn off the lights, use a simple eye mask. Turn the lights back up to full brightness when you wake up.

4. **Use a blanket.** When you sleep, your metabolism falls, your breathing rate slows, and your body temperature drops slightly. Though not imperative, you will usually be more comfortable if you use a light blanket when you nap.

5. **Be discreet.** Getting caught napping at your desk is not a good way to earn respect. In some old-school environments, it might even get you fired! But most people get an hour for lunch. Eat in half that time and then go snooze in your car, an unused conference room, or even a closet.

Finally, shift your own thinking about naps. People who take them are not lazy. They might just be the smartest, most productive people you know.

This material was obtained from *The Guardian News and Media Ltd*, Kings Place, 90 Yorkway, London N1 9GU, Inkd.in/XFcpCs, and reprinted with their consent.

Healthy Eating – Do's and Don'ts
On and Off the Job

Eat every 4-5 hours during the day: Breakfast, lunch, dinner and bedtime snack.

Eat about the same amount of food at each meal: 3-5 carbohydrate servings per meal.

Eat a wide variety of foods each meal: Some carbohydrates, proteins and fats, but especially free vegetables (those high in water or fiber).

Eat foods higher in fiber: Whole grains, fruits and vegetables. Remember this for snacking also.

Eat foods lower in fat: Skim milk, low fat cheeses, lean meats. Bake, broil, boil, grill rather than fry.

Eat foods lower in salt (sodium): 500 milligrams or less per meal is best.

Snack on low sodium nuts and seeds for beneficial nutrients.

Read the food labels: Look for total carbohydrates.

DON'T skip meals. This is especially true for the breakfast meal. Some breakfast foods can become very good snacks while on the job also. Find them and use to your advantage.

KEEP healthy snacks with you all day long and use as needed.

Partially adapted from the Veterans Administration

Five Steps to Total Relaxation and Reduction of Tension

These five steps can be used almost anywhere and at any time. They were adapted from some of the work done in this field by Dr. Edward S. Rosenbluh (1981, 1986). During total relaxation, your mind remains alert. As long as you do not do the steps for longer than twenty minutes, you are not likely to fall asleep. When you are finished, you will feel relaxed and fresh. Experienced relaxers even talk of a "natural high" produced without drugs.

When time or circumstances do not permit following the whole program, you may do parts of it. It can be done with your eyes open or shut. It can be done for short periods of time. It can even be done in a meeting, as a passenger in a car, during breaks or down-time, and during other appropriate or private times. You will feel more refreshed and alert even after a short session than if you had remained tense the entire time.

Step One: Sit or lie in a comfortable position. Allow the weight of all parts of your body to be supported. Lean your head forward if sitting, or back if lying down.

Step Two: Close your eyes and relax all parts of your body. Feel your feet getting heavy and relaxed, then your ankles, knees, hips, mid-section, hand, arms, shoulders, neck, jaw, eyes, forehead, and even your tongue. Feel each part of your body, in succession, starting with your feet, become heavy, relaxed and comfortable.

Step Three: Begin to concentrate on your breathing. Observe it with your mind as it slowly goes in and out. During each exhale, say the word, "One," to yourself; e.g., inhale, exhale, "One," inhale, exhale, "One."

Step Four: The word "One" will help keep meaningful thoughts from your mind. Do not worry if fleeting thoughts come in and out of focus. Concentrate on breathing and on "One."

Step Five: Continue for 20 minutes. Do this once in the morning and once in the evening, as needed and as possible. Do these steps anytime you feel tense. You may check the clock periodically. Because of digestion, which might interfere, it would probably be best to avoid total relaxation for about two hours after eating. If you feel your hands getting warmer, this is okay. Such sensations often accompany total relaxation. Sometimes, it even helps to think about your hands and arms getting warmer after Step Two.

(Rosenbluh, 1981, 1986 and Greenstone, 2008)

Relaxation – Its Benefits and How to Use It in a Crisis

There are several kinds of relaxation that will help return your stress levels to an acceptable place when you serve as an intervener. These routines will also be successful calming victims at the scene or after removing them from immediate danger. For example, you will find that working with a small group of folks at a shelter will help them unwind enough to be able to begin to process the event. On the other hand, have your partner read a relaxation script to help you return to a state of calm where you can do the most good for the victims. These techniques focus on the mind/body connection, understanding that one cannot be separated from another.

Types of Relaxation Techniques

- **Breathing** is the easiest body-only relaxation technique. Sustained deep breathing can counter the effects of a crisis and the effects of the stress response.

- **Stretching** is a natural. Have the participant concentrate on the place where he or she feels the most tension.

- **Systematic progressive relaxation** involves the intentional tightening and release of the muscles in the body. Each muscle group is attended to individually. Folks will become more aware of where they feel their stress and will eventually be able to address it more easily.

- **Passive progressive relaxation** systematically attends to tension in the various muscle groups of the body. It uses mental images to visualize the draining away of tension from the muscles. It takes some practice before deep relaxation is achieved.

- **Autogenic relaxation** combines deep breathing with images of draining or melting away stress as opposed to tightening and relaxing muscles. It suggests control and mastery of stress and is a good technique for someone who is feeling powerless.

- **Meditation** is somewhat like day dreaming with a purpose. The participant clears his or her mind and then concentrates on a single mental focus.

- **Guided imagery and visualization** takes advantage of the marvelous capacity of the mind to imagine and create sensory images. Participants may be taken to the sea, to the mountains, for a gentle canoe trip. Be careful to choose images that won't increase the anxiety already brought on by the crisis. Tell the participants that they may open their eyes and come back to reality if the images are uncomfortable.

- **Yoga** is a system of meditations and exercises. It is best left to the professional to use with crisis survivors.

Begin your relaxation session with a simple breathing exercise. This one is taken from *30 Scripts for Relaxation Imagery and & Inner Healing, Second Edition*, by Julie Lusk, and used by permission of Whole Person Associates. It works very well.

Breathing for Relaxation and Health
By Julie Lusk

Time: 10 minutes

Effective relaxation requires proper breathing. In this script, participants concentrate on their breathing by focusing on what their bodies feel like as they take in deep breaths, hold them briefly, and slowly exhale.

Note: The following information will help your participants understand the importance of slow, deep, rhythmic breathing. You may wish to present it as an introduction before using this script.

Breathe in and out through the nose, not the mouth, unless directed otherwise. The nose filters out pollutants and moistens and warms the air.

Breathing should be natural, smooth, easy, slow, quiet and complete. Exhaling fully and deeply is the first step to better breathing. It stimulates the functioning of the brain cells and rids the system of stale air. Exhaling helps activate the relaxation response via the parasympathetic nervous system and it lowers the heart rate. Exhaling fully creates ample room for the inhalation. More importantly, taking time for fully inhaling and exhaling slows the breathing rate down. Slowing the breathing rate down causes the brain to get more oxygen. This results in heightened awareness, increased alertness, and calmness. It diffuses anxiety and nervousness.

Oxygenation of the body is essential to physical health and well-being. Breathing abdominally rather than chest breathing, results in a greater transfer of oxygen into the blood for better delivery of nutrients to the tissues. Cells utilize oxygen to create energy. Oxygen is necessary for the development of all organs in the body. Red blood cells are completely renewed every 120 days. The most essential element for accomplishing this reconstruction is not food, but oxygen.

Shallow and irregular breathing can result in the accumulation of bodily wastes and toxins and inadequate functioning of all body organs and tissues. It is also an indicator of stress. Breathing that is slow, smooth, and deep helps alleviate these issues and leads to a clear and alert mind. It also improves the flow of lymph which can improve the immunity system.

Script

Close your eyes ... and bring your attention to your breathing ... It's time to begin following the air as it comes in ... and as it goes out while breathing through your nose.

Continue feeling your breath each time it comes in ... and as it goes out ... If your mind begins to wander, just bring it back to feeling and sensing your breath.

Notice if you can feel movement in your belly...your ribs...and your collar-bone while breathing naturally. Take your time.

Pause.

During the next several cycles of breathing, empty your lungs more than usual each time you breathe out. Let all the air out, compressing your stomach to squeeze out all the stale air and carbon dioxide ... Letting it all empty out.

Each time you breathe in, take in a nice, full, deep breath and let the air go all the way to the bottom of your lungs. Feel your stomach rise, your chest expand, and the collar-bone area fill.

As you breathe in, your diaphragm expands and massages all the internal organs in the abdominal area ... this helps digestion.

As you breathe out, relax ... Allowing any tension or knots in your belly to naturally untie ... To let go.

Breathing in ... Fully and completely.

Breathing out ... Letting it all go ... relaxing more and more ... Breathing heals you ... calms you ... it's soothing.

When breathing in fully and completely. Oxygen is entering your blood stream, and nourishes all your organs and cells. It protects you.

Breathing out releases metabolic waste and toxins. Your breath is cleansing you ... healing you.

Let's use the breath in another way and take advantage of the mind-body connection.

Leaders note: Use one or more of the following, depending on the group's needs or time available. Give participants enough time to experience this.

If you wish, imagine exhaling confusion … and inhaling clarity.

Imagine exhaling darkness … and inhaling light.

Imagine exhaling fear … and inhaling love.

Exhaling pain…and inhaling relief.

Exhaling anxiety … and inhaling peace.

Exhaling selfishness … and inhaling generosity.

Exhaling guilt … and inhaling forgiveness.

You may continue on with a guided meditation. If you choose to end here, repeat the following until everyone is alert.

Stretch and open your eyes, feeling refreshed, rejuvenated, alert, and fully alive.

The following is also from Julie Lusk's book, *30 Scripts for Relaxation Imagery & Inner Healing Second Edition* and used by permission from Whole Person Associates. It is an easy guided imagery with which to start.

Sun Meditation for Healing
By Judy Fulop and Julie Lusk

Time: 10 minutes

In this script, participants experience the healing power and energy of the sun as they imagine it warming and relaxing them.

Script

Please close your eyes and take some time to go within yourself to settle your body, mind, and heart. Feel free to use whatever method works best for you. For example, it may be focusing on your breath, meditating, stretching your body mindfully, or using a sound, word, image, or a phrase as a mantra to become centered … Take your time … allowing yourself to become more and more at ease with yourself.

Pause.

Allow yourself to become as relaxed and comfortable as you can ... Let your body feel supported by the ground underneath you.

Slowly begin to see or feel yourself lying in a grassy meadow with the sun shining its golden rays gently upon you ... Let yourself soak in these warm rays ... taking in the healing power and life giving energy of the sunshine.

This magnificent ball of light has been a sustaining source of energy for millions of years and will be an energy source for millions of years to come ... This ancient sun is the same sun which shined down upon the dinosaurs ... upon the Egyptians while they built the pyramids ... and it now shines upon the earth and all the other planets in our solar system and will continued to do so.

As the sun's rays gently touch your skin, allow yourself to feel the warmth and energy flow slowly through your body ... pulsing through your bones ... sending healing light to your organs ... flowing to your tissues ... recharging every system ... and now settling into your innermost being ... your heart center.

Sense your heart center glowing with this radiant energy. If you wish, give it a color ... Take a few moments to allow this warm and healing energy to reach your innermost being ... physically ... emotionally ... mentally ... and spiritually.

Pause for 30 seconds.

As this healing energy grows and expands, allow yourself to see, feel, and sense this energy surrounding your being ... growing and growing ... Allow this energy to further fill this room ... this building ... surrounding this town ... spreading throughout our state ... to our country ... and out into the worlds ... and finally throughout the universe ... reaching and touching and blessing all.

Pause for 30 seconds.

You may share this healing energy and power with anyone you're aware of right now ... Mentally ask them if they are willing to receive this healing energy ... If they are ... send this source of healing energy to them ... giving them the time they need to take in this energy and make it theirs in their own heart center.

Pause for 30 seconds.

Now take your attention back to your own heart center ... Find a safe place within you to keep this healing and powerful energy ... a place to keep it protected and within your reach ... Give yourself permission to get in touch with this energy whenever you wish.

With the warmth of this energy in your being, begin stretching, wiggling, and moving ... Slowly open your eyes, feeling alive, refreshed, keenly alert, and completely healthy.

Repeat the above instructions until everyone is alert.

Table 1. Officers' perceptual distortions during shooting incidents (n = 113)

Distortion	At any time	Prior to firing	Upon firing
Tunnel vision	51%	31%	27%
Heightened visual detail	56%	37%	35%
Both visual distortions	15%	10%	11%
Auditory blunting	82%	42%	70%
Auditory acuity	20%	10%	5%
Both aural distortions	9%	0%	9%
Slow motion	56%	43%	40%
Fast motion	23%	12%	17%
Both time distortions	2%	0%	2%
Other	13%	6%	9%
Total	95%	88%	94%

Table 2. Officers' responses following a shooting

Physical response	At any time (n = 113)	First 24 hours (n = 112)	First week (n = 113)	Within 3 months (n = 111)	After 3 months (n = 105)
Trouble sleeping	48%	46%	36%	16%	11%
Fatigue	46%	39%	26%	7%	5%
Crying	24%	17%	7%	2%	2%
Appetite loss	17%	16%	8%	2%	1%
Headache	7%	6%	4%	1%	1%
Nausea	4%	4%	4%	0%	0%
Other physical response	19%	18%	11%	12%	6%
Thoughts and feelings					
Recurrent thoughts	83%	82%	74%	52%	37%
Anxiety	40%	37%	28%	13%	10%
Fear of legal or administrative problems	34%	31%	25%	19%	11%
Elation	29%	26%	19%	11%	5%
Sadness	26%	18%	17%	5%	5%
Numbness	20%	18%	7%	4%	3%
Nightmares	18%	13%	13%	10%	6%
Fear for safety	18%	9%	10%	9%	8%
Guilt	12%	10%	5%	6%	2%
Other thoughts or feelings	42%	33%	23%	20%	14%

Note: The different n values reflect the timing of the 113 shootings. For example, two of the shootings occurred within 3 weeks before the interview and another six occurred between 2 and 3 months before the interviews. One officer was critically injured and unconscious for 48 hours following her shooting, so questions regarding the first 24 hours after her shooting did not apply to her.

What Happens in the Months Following a Shooting?

Most officers reported experiencing no negative reactions three months after the shooting, and fewer than one in five reported "severe" reactions (two or more negative emotional or physical reactions) three months after the shooting. Even in the short term, many officers experienced no or only one negative reaction during the first day and week following a shooting (38 and 52 percent, respectively). Only one specific reaction—recurrent thoughts—persisted past the 3-month mark in more than one-third of the cases, and only two other reactions exceeded 10 percent—fear of legal problems and trouble sleeping, both of which were reported in 11 percent of the cases.

The emotions that officers experienced were not all negative. Following about one-third of the shootings, officers reported feelings of elation that included joy at being alive, residual excitement after a life-threatening situation, and satisfaction or pride in proving their ability to use deadly force appropriately.

Expressions of support from fellow officers, detailed discussions about the incident with officers who had previously shot a suspect, and taking department-mandated time off following the shooting were associated with slight or moderate reductions in officers' negative reactions. Conversely, officers who felt a lack of support from their colleagues and supervisors or that aspects of the investigation into the shooting were unfair or unprofessional reported more severe and longer-lasting negative reactions following the shooting, particularly after three months. Less predictably, support from intimate partners or family members and attendance at mandatory mental health counseling sessions were not associated with officers' postshooting reactions.

What Does This Mean for Police Agencies?

Training. The finding that most officers in this study experienced little long-term disruption as a result of shooting a suspect calls into question the appropriateness of training that stresses the severe guilt and depression felt by some officers who shoot. Focusing on severe responses that occur infrequently may be misleading and counterproductive. Several officers indicated in interviews that they thought something might be wrong with them because they did not experience the symptoms that training taught them to expect; others felt that, through the power of suggestion, their reactions were more severe than they would have been otherwise.

Mental health counseling. Many officers who underwent mandatory postshooting counseling reported that the experience was not positive (although three officers who reported long-term depression found counseling to be helpful). Most officers who held this opinion said they believed their department required counseling to shield itself from legal liability, not to help the officers themselves. They stated that they did not talk frankly to the counselors because they did not trust them to keep the sessions confidential; in some cases, they thought the counselors were incompetent.

Several officers admitted that they lied to counselors about their reactions because they did not want to divulge their thoughts, feelings, and experiences to a stranger with ties to the department. This contrasts with officers' willingness to discuss the shooting with fellow officers who had also been involved in shootings and suggests that peer counseling may be more helpful to these officers than mandatory critical incident debriefings.

Officers may honestly say they cannot recall some aspect of the incident or report information that conflicts with other evidence. Investigators faced with problematic statements from officers can try to fill in the gaps or reconcile conflicting evidence through further investigation.

In addition, because officers may fire at a suspect without realizing it, investigators may want to check the weapons of all officers who were immediately present at a shooting for evidence of firing, even if the officers report that they did not fire.

Retrieved from nij.gov/journals/253/pages/responses.aspx April 6, 2015.

Suicide

The person who is suicidal is not moving toward death.

- The suicidal person is trying very hard to move away from their own life the way it is; with all of the pain and humiliation that they are experiencing, and with no other apparent way out.

- Suicide is not about death. It is about real conflict, either internal or external, between at least one other person or institution either present or absent in the sufferer's life at that time.

- Often what the suicidal individual needs is a real way out of the conflict or humiliation other than the suicidal act. Platitudes will not help.

- 90% of people who die by suicide have a diagnosable and treatable psychiatric disorder at the time of their death, most often depression and/or alcohol/substance abuse.

- Most people with mental illness do not die by suicide.

- Yearly medical costs for suicide are at nearly $100 million (2005).

Common misconceptions

- "People who talk about suicide won't really do it." Almost everyone who commits or attempts suicide has given some clue or warning. Do not ignore suicide threats. Statements like "You'll be sorry when I'm dead," "I can't see any way out," – no matter how casually or jokingly said, may indicate serious suicidal feelings.

- "Anyone who tries to kill him/herself must be crazy." Most suicidal people are not psychotic or insane. They may be upset, grief-stricken, depressed or despairing. Extreme distress and emotional pain are always signs of mental illness but are not signs of psychosis.

- "If a person is determined to kill him/herself, nothing is going to stop him/her." Even the most severely depressed person has mixed feelings about death, and most waiver until the very last moment between wanting to live and wanting to end their pain. Most suicidal people do not want to die; they want the pain to stop. The impulse to end it all, however overpowering, does not last forever. The usual cause (depression) can be treated.

- "People who commit suicide are people who were unwilling to seek help." Studies of adult suicide victims have shown that more than half had sought medical help within six months before their deaths and a majority had seen a medical professional within 1 month of their death.

- "Talking about suicide may give someone the idea." You don't give a suicidal person ideas by talking about suicide. The opposite is true –

bringing up the subject of suicide and discussing it openly is one of the most helpful things you can do. You are providing them with a safe opportunity to express their feelings and to have an ally in seeking help.

Warning signs
- Threatening suicide or self-harm
- Looking for ways to kill oneself (weapons, pills or other means)
- Talking or writing about death, dying or suicide
- Feeling desperate or trapped
- Feelings of hopelessness
- Feeling there is no reason or purpose to live
- Expressing rage, intense anger or seeking revenge
- Feelings of intense anxiety or panic
- Acting reckless or engaging in risky activities
- Increasing alcohol or drug use
- Withdrawing from friends or family

Risk Factors

Any of the following risk factors means the person is more vulnerable to suicide than the average person. In general, the presence of more risk factors means higher risk.

- Psychiatric and medical illnesses: Depression, bipolar disorder, alcohol/drug abuse, schizophrenia, seizure disorders, multiple sclerosis, any serious illness
- History of previous suicide attempt(s), trauma or abuse, family suicide
- Recent stress: Suicide of friend, acquaintance or someone in the community; loss of a relationship; failure or humiliation
- Access to method: Especially to guns, but also drugs, high buildings, etc.

Fatal suicidal behavior
- In previous years, suicide was the 10th leading cause of death for all ages.
- In 2009, the suicide rate increased 2.4% over 2008 to equal approximately 12 suicides per 100,000 people. The rate has been increasing since 2000. This the highest rate of suicide in 15 years.
- More than 36,000 suicides occurred in the U.S. This is the equivalent of 94 suicides per day; one suicide every 14.2 minutes or 12.0 suicides per 100,000 population.
- Every year, there are almost twice as many suicides as homicides.

- The National Violent Death Reporting System includes information on the presence of alcohol and other substances at the time of death. For those tested for substances, the findings from the 16 states revealed that one-third of those who died by suicide were positive for alcohol at the time of death and nearly 1 in 5 had evidence of opiates, including heroin and prescription pain killers.

Nonfatal suicidal thoughts and behavior

- Among young adults ages 15-24 years old, there are approximately 100-200 attempts for every completed suicide.

- Among adults ages 65 years and older, there are approximately four suicide attempts for every completed suicide.

- In previous years, 13.8% of U.S. high school students reported that they had seriously considered attempting suicide during the 12 months preceding the survey; 6.3% of students reported that they had actually attempted suicide one or more times during the same period.
- Nearly 1,000,000 people make a suicide attempt every year.

Gender Disparities

- Males take their own lives at nearly four times the rate of females and represent 78.8% of all U.S. suicides.

- During their lifetime, women attempt suicide about two to three times as often as men.

- Suicide is the seventh leading cause of death for males and the fifteenth leading cause for females.

- Suicide rates for males are highest among those aged 75 and older (rate 36.1 per 100,000).

- Suicide rates for females are highest among those aged 45-54 (rate 8.8 per 100,000 population).

- Firearms are the most commonly used method of suicide among males (55.7%).
- Poisoning is the most common method of suicide for females (40.2%).

Racial and Ethnic Disparities

- Among American Indians/Alaska Natives ages 15-34 years, suicide is the second leading cause of death.

- Suicide rates among American Indian/Alaskan Native adolescents and young adults ages 15-34 (20.0 per 100,000) are 1.8 times higher than the national average for that age group (11.4 per 100,000).

- Hispanic and Black, non-Hispanic female high school students in grades 9-12 reported a higher percentage of suicide attempts (11.1% and 10.4%, respectively) than their White, non-Hispanic counterparts (6.5%).

Age Group Differences

- Suicide is the second leading cause of death among 25-34 year olds and the third leading cause of death among 15-24 year olds.
- Among 15-24 year olds, suicide accounts for 12.2% of all deaths annually.
- The rate of suicide for adults aged 75 years and older was 16.0 per 100,000.

Nonfatal, Self-Inflicted Injuries

- Yearly rates show that 376,306 people were treated in emergency departments for self-inflicted injuries.
- Yearly rates indicate that 163,489 people were hospitalized due to self-inflicted injury.
- There is one suicide for every 25 attempted suicides.

Suicide-Related Behaviors among U.S. High School Students

In one representative year:

- 13.8% of students in grades 9-12 seriously considered suicide in the previous 12 months (17.4% of females and 10.5% of males).
- 6.3% of students reported making at least one suicide attempt in the previous 12 months (8.1% of females and 4.6% of males).
- 1.9% of students had made a suicide attempt that resulted in an injury, poisoning, or an overdose that required medical attention (2.5% of females and 1.6% of males).

Suicide and United States Armed Forces Troops:
Abstracted Facts

1. Suicides in 2012 averaged one per day.

2. In 2012, there were 154 suicides in the first 155 days of the year.

3. Sexual assaults, alcohol abuse and domestic violence are occurring in increasing numbers.

4. Suicide rates leveled off in 2010 and 2011.

5. To try to explain the suicide rates, studies have pointed to:
   Combat exposure
   Post trauma stress
   Misuse of prescription medications
   Personal financial problems
   Multiple combat tours

6. A substantial number of Army suicides were committed by soldiers who never deployed.

7. The 2012 active-duty suicide total, through June 3, is 154. The same period in 2011 was 130 suicides. This is an 18% increase in suicides.

8. 2012's January – May total is up 25% from 2010 and is 16% above 2009.

9. Suicide rates have exceeded U.S. combat deaths in Afghanistan for 2009, 2010 and 2011.

10. There are 1.4 million active-duty military personnel.

11. Seeking help for mental health problems is still largely seen as a sign of weakness.

12. The weaker economy may be a confounding factor in preventative efforts for suicide.

13. Signs of suicide may show up more dramatically when fighting goes down and the Army is returning to garrison.

14. Opinions are that many senior military officers do not grasp the nature of the suicide problem.

15. U.S. Marine Corps have the most success in lowering their suicide rates.
    Marines: Slightly up in 2012.

Army: Up slightly.
Air Force: Spike to 32 through 3 June 2012.
Navy: Slightly above the 10 year trend but down from 2011.

16. Most suicidal people are not psychotic.

17. Suicidal people may be upset, grief-stricken, depressed or despairing.

18. Impact of Army suicide prevention program is unknown.

19. Suicide numbers began surging in 2006.

20. Suicide numbers soared in 2009 and leveled off before climbing in 2012.

21. Numbers do not include National Guard or Reserve members.

Material compiled by COL James L. Greenstone.

Commonly Abused Drugs Chart

Tobacco

Category & Name	Examples of Commercial & Street Names	DEA Schedule	How Administered*
Nicotine	Found in cigarettes, cigars, bidis and smokeless tobacco (snuff, spit tobacco, chew)	Not scheduled	Smoked, snorted, chewed

Acute Effects – Increased blood pressure and heart rate

Health Risks – Chronic lung disease; cardiovascular disease; stroke; cancers of the mouth, pharynx, larynx, esophagus, stomach, pancreas, cervix, kidney, bladder, and acute myeloid leukemia; adverse pregnancy outcomes; addiction

Alcohol

Category & Name	Examples of Commercial & Street Names	DEA Schedule	How Administered*
Alcohol (ethyl alcohol)	Found in liquor, beer and wine	Not scheduled	Swallowed

Acute Effects – In low doses, euphoria, mild stimulation, relaxation, lowered inhibitions; in higher doses, drowsiness, slurred speech, nausea, emotional volatility, loss of coordination, visual distortions, impaired memory, sexual dysfunction, loss of consciousness

Health Risks – Increased risk of injuries, violence, fetal damage (in pregnant women); depression; neurologic deficits; hypertension; liver and heart disease; addiction; fatal overdose

Cannabinoids

Category & Name	Examples of Commercial & Street Names	DEA Schedule	How Administered*
Marijuana	Blunt, dope, ganja, grass, herb, joint, bud, Mary Jane, pot, reefer, green, trees, smoke, sinsemilla, skunk, weed	I?	Smoked, swallowed
Hashish	Boom, gangster, hash, hash oil, hemp	I?	Smoked, swallowed

Acute Effects – Euphoria; relaxation; slowed reaction time; distorted sensory perception; impaired balance and coordination; increased heart rate and appetite; impaired learning, memory; anxiety; panic attacks; psychosis

Health Risks – Cough, frequent respiratory infections; possible mental health decline; addiction

Opioids

Category & Name	Examples of Commercial & Street Names	DEA Schedule	How Administered*
Heroin	*Diacetylmorphine:* smack, horse, brown sugar, dope, H, junk, skag, skunk, white horse, China white; cheese (with OTC cold medicine and antihistamine)	I?	Injected, smoked, snorted
Opium	*Laudanum, paregoric:* big O, black stuff, block, gum, hop	II, III, V?	Swallowed, smoked

Acute Effects – Euphoria; drowsiness; impaired coordination; dizziness; confusion; nausea; sedation; feeling of heaviness in the body; slowed or arrested breathing

Health Risks – Constipation; endocarditis; hepatitis; HIV; addiction; fatal overdose

Stimulants

Category & Name	Examples of Commercial & Street Names	DEA Schedule	How Administered*
Cocaine	*Cocaine hydrochloride:* blow, bump, C, candy, Charlie, coke, crack, flake, rock, snow, toot	II?	Snorted, smoked, injected
Amphetamine	*Biphetamine, Dexedrine:* bennies, black beauties, crosses, hearts, LA turnaround, speed, truck drivers, uppers	II?	Swallowed, snorted, smoked, injected
Methamphetamine	*Desoxyn:* meth, ice, crank, chalk, crystal, fire, glass, go fast, speed	II?	Swallowed, snorted, smoked, injected

Acute Effects – Increased heart rate, blood pressure, body temperature, metabolism; feelings of exhilaration; increased energy, mental alertness; tremors; reduced appetite; irritability; anxiety; panic; paranoia; violent behavior; psychosis

Health Risks – Weight loss, insomnia; cardiac or cardiovascular complications; stroke; seizures; addiction

Also, for cocaine – Nasal damage from snorting

Also, for methamphetamine – Severe dental problems

Club Drugs

Category & Name	Examples of Commercial & Street Names	DEA Schedule	How Administered*
MDMA (methylenedioxy-methamphetamine)	Ecstasy, Adam, clarity, Eve, lover's speed, peace, uppers	I?	Swallowed, snorted, injected
Flunitrazepam	*Rohypnol:* forget-me pill, Mexican Valium, R2, roach, Roche, roofies, roofinol, rope, rophies	IV?	Swallowed, snorted
GHB	Georgia home boy, grievous bodily harm, liquid ecstasy, soap, scoop, goop, liquid X	I?	Swallowed

Acute Effects, for MDMA – Mild hallucinogenic effects; increased tactile sensitivity; empathic feelings; lowered inhibition; anxiety; chills; sweating; teeth clenching; muscle cramping

Also, for Flunitrazepam – Sedation; muscle relaxation; confusion; memory loss; dizziness; impaired coordination

Also, for GHB – Drowsiness; nausea; headache; disorientation; loss of coordination; memory loss

Health Risks, for MDMA – Sleep disturbances; depression; impaired memory; hyperthermia; addiction

Also, for Flunitrazepam – Addiction

Also, for GHB – Unconsciousness; seizures; coma

Dissociative Drugs

Category & Name	Examples of Commercial & Street Names	DEA Schedule	How Administered*
Ketamine	*Ketalar SV:* cat Valium, K, Special K, vitamin K	III?	Snorted, smoked, injected
PCP and analogs	*Phencyclidine:* angel dust, boat, hog, love boat, peace pill	I, II?	Swallowed, smoked, injected
Salvia divinorum	Salvia, Shepherdess's Herb, Maria Pastora, magic mint, Sally-D	Not scheduled	Chewed, swallowed, smoked
Dextromethorphan (DXM)	Found in some cough and cold medications: Robotripping, Robo, Triple C	Not scheduled	Swallowed

Acute Effects – Feelings of being separate from one's body and environment; impaired motor function

Also, for Ketamine – Analgesia; impaired memory; delirium; respiratory depression and arrest; death

Also, for PCP and analogs – Analgesia; psychosis; aggression; violence; slurred speech; loss of coordination; hallucinations

Also, for DXM – Euphoria; slurred speech; confusion; dizziness; distorted visual perceptions

Health Risks – Anxiety; tremors; numbness; memory loss; nausea

Hallucinogens

Category & Name	Examples of Commercial & Street Names	DEA Schedule	How Administered*
LSD	*Lysergic acid diethylamide:* acid, blotter, cubes, microdot yellow sunshine, blue heaven	I?	Swallowed, absorbed through mouth tissues
Mescaline	Buttons, cactus, mesc, peyote	I?	Swallowed, smoked
Psilocybin	Magic mushrooms, purple passion, shrooms, little smoke	I?	Swallowed

Acute Effects – Altered states of perception and feeling; hallucinations; nausea

Also, for LSD – Increased body temperature, heart rate, blood pressure; loss of appetite; sweating; sleeplessness; numbness, dizziness, weakness, tremors; impulsive behavior; rapid shifts in emotion

Also, for Mescaline – Increased body temperature, heart rate, blood pressure; loss of appetite; sweating; sleeplessness; numbness, dizziness, weakness, tremors; impulsive behavior; rapid shifts in emotion

Also, for Psilocybin – Nervousness; paranoia; panic

Health Risks, for LSD – Flashbacks, Hallucinogen Persisting Perception Disorder

Other Compounds

Category & Name	Examples of Commercial & Street Names	DEA Schedule	How Administered*
Anabolic steroids	*Anadrol, Oxandrin, Durabolin, Depo-Testosterone, Equipoise:* roids, juice, gym candy, pumpers	III?	Swallowed, injected, applied to skin
Inhalants	Solvents (paint thinners, gasoline, glues); gases (butane, propane, aerosol propellants, nitrous oxide); nitrites (isoamyl, isobutyl, cyclohexyl): laughing gas, poppers, snappers, whippets	Not scheduled	Inhaled through nose or mouth

Acute Effects, for Anabolic steroids – No intoxication effects

Also, for Inhalants (varies by chemical) – Stimulation; loss of inhibition; headache; nausea or vomiting; slurred speech; loss of motor coordination; wheezing

Health Risks, for Anabolic steroids – Hypertension; blood clotting and cholesterol changes; liver cysts; hostility and aggression; acne, in adolescents – premature stoppage of growth; in males – prostate cancer, reduced sperm production, shrunken testicles, breast enlargement; in females – menstrual irregularities, development of beard and other masculine characteristics

Also, for Inhalants – Cramps; muscle weakness; depression; memory impairment; damage to cardiovascular and nervous systems; unconsciousness; sudden death

Prescription Medications

Category & Name	Examples of Commercial & Street Names	DEA Schedule	How Administered*
CNS Depressants Stimulants Opioid Pain Relievers	For more information on prescription medications, please see below		

Facts about Prescription Drug Abuse

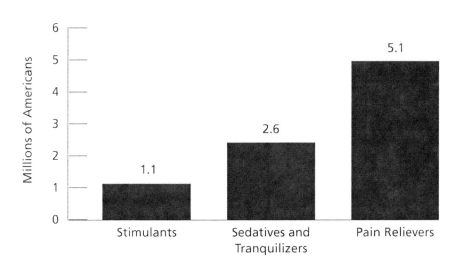

About 7 Million Americans Reported Past-Month Use of Prescription Drugs for Nonmedical Purposes in 2010

Three types of drugs are abused most often:

- Opioids – prescribed for pain relief
- CNS depressants – barbiturates and benzodiazepines prescribed for anxiety or sleep problems (often referred to as sedatives or tranquilizers)
- Stimulants – prescribed for attention-deficit hyperactivity disorder (ADHD), the sleep disorder narcolepsy, or obesity.

Prevalence of Past-Year Drug Use Among 12th Graders

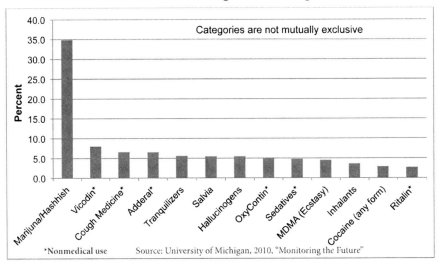

*Nonmedical use   Source: University of Michigan, 2010, "Monitoring the Future"

Prescription and Nonmedical use of Over-the-Counter Medication Account for Most of the Commonly Abused Drugs

How can you help prevent prescription drug abuse?

- Ask your doctor or pharmacist about your medication, especially if you are unsure about its effects
- Keep your doctor informed about all medications you are taking, including over-the-counter medications.
- Read the information your pharmacist provides before starting to take medications.
- Take your medication(s) as prescribed.
- Keep all prescription medications secured at all times and properly dispose of any unused medications.

*Some of the health risks are directly related to the route of drug administration. For example, injection drug use can increase the risk of infection through needle contamination with staphylococci, HIV, hepatitis and other organisms.

**Associated with sexual assaults

Principles of Drug Addiction Treatment

More than three decades of scientific research show that treatment can help drug-addicted individuals stop drug use, avoid relapse and successfully recover their lives. Based on this research, 13 fundamental principles that characterize effective drug abuse treatment have been developed. These principles are detailed in NIDA's Principles of Drug Addiction Treatment: A Research-Based Guide. The guide also describes different types of science-based treatments and provides answers to commonly asked questions.

National Institute on Drug Abuse, National Institutes of Health

Appendix C
References

Advanced disaster life support (2006). National Disaster Life Support Foundation. Chicago: American Medical Association.

Agency for Healthcare Research and Quality. (2005). Altered standards of care in mass casualty events. AHRQ Publication No. 05-0043, April 2005. Washington, DC: U.S. Department of Health and Human Services. http://www.ahrq.gov.

Beevers, C.G., et al. (March 31, 2011). Association of predeployment gaze bias for emotional stimuli with later symptoms of PTSD and depression in soldiers deployed in Iraq. American Journal of Psychiatry. Retrieved June 7, 2011 from http://dx.doi.org/10.1176/appi.ajp.2011.10091309.

Centers for Disease Control, National Institute for Occupational Safety and Health. (2002). Emergency response workers: Traumatic stress incidence. Atlanta, Georgia: Author. Retrieved December 28, 2010, from http://www.cdc.gov/niosh/docs/2002-107/.

Certification commission for healthcare interpreters. (2010). Retrieved from http://www.healthcareinterpretercertification.org.

Disaster Mental Health Services, Substance Abuse and Mental Health Services Administration (SAMHSA). (2002). Self-care tips for emergency and disaster response workers, SAMHSA. Washington, D.C.: Author.

DiVasto, P.V. (June, 1996). Negotiating with foreign language-speaking subjects. The FBI Law Enforcement Bulletin, 65(6), 6-10.

Evarts, W.R., Greenstone, J.L, Kirkpatrick, G.J. and Leviton, S.C. (1983). Winning through accommodation: The mediator's handbook. Dubuque, Iowa: Kendall/Hunt Publishing Company.

Greenstone, J.L. (Fall, 2011). Tactical combat casualty care training for state defense forces medical units. Journal of the State Defense Forces Publication Center, 6(1), 20-25.

Greenstone, J.L. (Spring, 2010). Use of interpreters with crisis intervention teams, behavioral health units and medical strike teams: Responding appropriately and effectively. International Journal of Emergency Mental Health, 12(2), 79-82.

Greenstone, J.L. (2008). The elements of disaster psychology: Managing psychosocial trauma – an integrated approach to force protection and acute care. Springfield, Illinois: Charles C. Thomas Publishers.

Greenstone, J.L. (1993). Critical incident stress debriefing and crisis management. Austin, TX: Texas Department of Health, Bureau of Emergency Management.

Greenstone, J.L. and Leviton, S.C. (1982). Crisis intervention: Handbook for interveners. Dubuque, Iowa: Kendall/Hunt Publishing Company.

Greenstone, J.L. and Leviton, S.C. (2010). Elements of crisis intervention: Crises and how to respond to them, (3rd Ed). Pacific Grove, CA: Brooks/Cole Publishing Company.

Greenstone, J.L. & Leviton, Sharon (1981). Hotline: Crisis intervention directory. New York: Facts on File.

Greenstone, J.L. (2005). The elements of police hostage and crisis negotiations: Critical incidents and how to respond to them. Binghamton, New York: The Haworth Press, Inc.

Groopman, J. (2007). How doctors think. New York: Houghton-Mifflin.

Holdeman, E. (2008). Disaster denial. Cowlitz County: Department of Emergency Management.

Personal equipment check list. (2010). Disaster Medical Assistance Team, TX-4. Retrieved January 6, 2011, from http://www.tx4dmat.org/Reference/personal_equipment.htm.

Reese, S.M. (2010, November 16). Exclusive ethics survey: Should I keep this patient alive? Medscape Medical Ethics. Retrieved November 23, 2010, from http:// www.medscape.com/viewarticle/731856.

Ripley, A. (August, 2006). Floods, tornadoes, hurricanes, wildfires, earthquakes: Why we don't prepare. Time Magazine, Vol. 168, No.8, (10-16).

Rosenbluh, E.S. (1981). Emotional first aid: Crises – their development and systems of intervention. Louisville, KY: American Academy of Crisis Interveners.

Rosenbluh, E.D. (1986). Crisis counseling: Emotional first aid. Dubuque, Iowa: Kendall/Hunt Publishing Company.

Schwartz, R., McManus, J. and Swienton, R. E. (2007). Tactical and operational emergency medical services command and support. Philadelphia, PA: Lippincott, Williams & Wilkins.

Sherif, M. and Sherif, C. (1948, 1956). An outline of social psychology. New York: Harper and Row Publishers.

The psychology of risk perception (June, 2011). Harvard Mental Health Letter. 27(12), 6.

Unconventional medic (2010). American Rescue Products, Incorporated.

Yun, K., et al. (September 23, 2010). Moving mental health into the disaster-preparedness spotlight. New England Journal of Medicine, 363 (13), 1193-1195.

Bibliography Specific to Resiliency

Armed forces health surveillance center (AFHSC): Update: deployment health assessments. (2009). U.S. Armed Forces Medical Surveillance Monthly Report, 16(10): 16-17.

Armed forces health surveillance center (AFHSC): Update: deployment health Assessments.(2009). U.S. Armed Forces Medical Surveillance Monthly Report, 17(1): 10-11.

Armed forces health surveillance center (AFHSC): Relationship between the nature and timing of mental disorders before and after deploying to Iraq/Afghanistan, active component. (2009). US Armed Forces Medical Surveillance Monthly Report (MSMR), 16(2): 2-6.

Armed forces health surveillance center: Ambulatory visits among members of active components, (2009). U.S. Armed Forces, 2008. Medical Surveillance Monthly Report, 16(4): 10-21.

Bliese P., Wright K., Adler A., Thomas J., & Hoge C. (2007). Timing of post-combat mental health assessments. Psychological Services, 4(3): 141-48.

Bowles, S.V., Bates, M.J.(2010). Military organizations and programs contributing to resilience building. Military Medicine, 175(6): 382-85.

Brummett, B.H., Boyle, S.H., Kuhn, C.M., Siegler, I.C., Williams, R.B. (2009). Positive affect is associated with cardiovascular reactivity, norepinephrine level, and morning rise in salivary cortisol. Psychophysiology, 46(4): 862-69.

Brydon, L., Walker, C., Wawrzyniak, A.J., Chart, H., Steptoe, A. (2009). Dispositional optimism and stress-induced changes in immunity and negative mood. Brain Behavioral Immunology, 23(6): 810-16.

Casey, L.M., Oei, T.P., Newcombe, P.A. (2004). An integrated cognitive model of panic disorder: The role of positive and negative cognitions. Clinical Psychology Review, 24(5): 529-55.

Chida, Y., Steptoe, A. (2008). Positive psychological well-being and mortality: A quantitative review of prospective observational studies. Psychosomatic Medicine, 70(7): 741-56.

Cigrang, J.A., Carbone, E.G, & Lara, A. (2003). Four-year prospective study of military trainees returned to duty following a mental health evaluation. Military Medicine, 168(9): 710-14.

Cigrang, J.A., Todd, S.L., Carbone, E.G. (2000). Stress management training for military trainees returned to duty after a mental health evaluation: Effect on graduation rates. Journal of Occupational Health Psychology, 5(1): 48-55.

Declercq ER, Bichell TJ, Center JK. (1997). Population-based needs assessment: Bringing public health to midwifery practice, Journal of Nurse Midwifery, 42(6): 478-88.

Department of the Army: Department of the Army Field Manual (FM) 4-02.51 (FM 8-51). Combat and Operational Stress Control. (2006). Retrieved from fas.org/irp/doddir/army/fm4-02-51.pdf.

Department of Defense (DoD): DoD Directive (DoDD) 6200.04, Force health Protection. (2007). Retrieved from http://www.dtic.mil/whs/directives/corres/pdf/620004p.pdf.

Diener, E., Oishi, S., Lucas, R.E. (2003). Personality, culture, and subjective well-being: Emotional and cognitive evaluations of life. Annual Review of Psychology, 54: 403-25.

Earvolino-Ramirez, M. (2007). Resilience: A concept analysis. Nursing Forum, 42(2): 73-82.

Firth, K. (2010). A survey of multidimensional health and fitness indexes. Military Medicine,175 (Suppl 1, August 2010): 110-17.

Folkman, S. (2008). The case for positive emotions in the stress process. Anxiety Stress Coping, 21(1): 3-14.

Garamone, J. (2005). Chairman calls for better mental health programs. American Forces Press Service, 1-2. Retrieved September 24, 2010, from http://www.defenselink.mil/news/newsarticle.aspx?id=5653.

Gold, M.A., Friedman, S.B. (2000). Cadet basic training: An ethnographic study of stress and coping. Military Medicine, 165(2): 147-52.

Greene-Shortridge, T.M., Britt, T.W., Castro, C.A. (2007). The stigma of mental health problems in the military. Military Medicine, 172(2): 157-61.

Hart, S.L., Vella, L., Mohr, D.C. (2008). Relationships among depressive symptoms, benefit-finding, optimism, and positive affect in multiple sclerosis patients after psychotherapy for depression. Health Psychology, 27(2): 230-38.

Hoge, C.W., Castro, C.A., Messer, S.C., McGurk, D., Cotting, D.I., Koffman, R.L. (2004). Combat duty in Iraq and Afghanistan, mental health problems, and barriers to care. New England Journal of Medicine, 351(1): 13-22.

Hourani, L.L., Williams, T.V., Kress, A.M. (2006). Stress, mental health, and job performance among active duty military personnel: Findings from the 2002 Department of Defense Health-

Related Behaviors Survey. Military Medicine., 171(9): 849-56.

Hourani LL, Yuan H, Bray RM. (2003). Psychosocial and health correlates of types of traumatic event exposures among US military personnel. Military Medicine, 168(9): 736-43.

Ice, G.H., James, G.D. (2007). Conducting a field study of stress: General principles. In Ice, G.H. & James, G.D., (Eds.), Measuring stress in humans: A practical guide for the field. Cambridge: Cambridge University Press, 1-24.

Institute of Medicine (IOM) Committee on the initial assessment of readjustment needs of military personnel, veterans, and their families board on the health of selected populations:

Preliminary assessment of readjustment needs of Veterans, service members, and their families.(2010). The National Academies Press. 2010.

Ironson, G., Hayward, H. (2008). Do positive psychosocial factors predict disease progression in HIV-1?: A review of the evidence. Psychosomatic Medicine, 70(5): 546-54.

Kindig D, Stoddart G. (2003). What is population health? American Journal of Public Health, 93(3): 380-83.

Lamkin, D.M,, Lutgendorf, S.K., McGinn, S., et al (2008). Positive psychosocial factors and NKT cells in ovarian cancer patients. Brain Behavioral Immunology, 22(1): 65-73.

Landry, L. (2008). Provider resiliency training (PRT): The most informative PRT overview in the briefest time span ever. Paper presented at the 2008 US Marine Corps Combat Operational Stress Conference, 28-30 May 2008, San Diego, CA. Retrieved August 29, 2010, from http://www.usmc-mccs.org/cosc/conference/sessions3.cfm.

LeardMann, C.A., Smith, T.C., Smith, B., Wells, T.S., Ryan M.A. (2009). Baseline self-reported functional health and vulnerability to post-traumatic stress disorder after combat deployment: Prospective US military cohort study. British Medical Journal, 338: b1273.

Logan, J.G., Barksdale, D.J. (2008). Allostasis and allostatic load: Expanding the discourse on stress and cardiovascular disease. Journal of Clinical Nursing, 17(7B): 201-208.

Lyon, B.L. (2000). Stress, coping and health: A conceptual overview. In Rice, V.H., (Ed.) Handbook of stress, coping, and health: implications for nursing research, theory, and practice. Thousand Oaks: Sage Publications; 3-26.

Lyubomirsky, S., King, L., Diener, E. (2005). The benefits of frequent positive affect: Does happiness lead to success? Psychological Bulletin, 131(6): 803-55.

Maguen, S., Turcotte, D.M., Peterson, A.L., et al. (2008). Description of risk and resilience factors among military medical personnel before deployment to Iraq. Military Medicine, 73(1): 1-9.

Martin, P.D., Williamson, D.A., Alfonso, A.J., & Ryan, D.H.(2006). Psychological adjustment during Army basic training. Military Medicine,171(2): 157-60.

Matthews, M.D. (2008). Toward a positive military psychology. Military Psychology. 20(4): 289-298.

Morgan, B.J. and Garmon Bibb, S.C. (In process, 2011). Assessment of the population-based psychological resilience needs of military personnel. Military Medicine, Unpublished.

Mullen, M. (2010).On total force fitness in war and peace. Military Medicine, 175(Suppl 1, August 2010): 1-2.

Ostir, G.V., Berges, I.M., Markides, K.S., Ottenbacher, K.J. (2006). Hypertension in older adults and the role of positive emotions. Psychosomatic Medicine, 68(5): 727-33.

Ostir, G.V., Berges, I.M., Ottenbacher, M.E., Clow, A., Ottenbacher, K.J. (2008). Associations between positive emotion and recovery of functional status following stroke. Psychosomatic Medicine, 70(4): 404-9.

Pollack, L.M., Boyer, C.B., Betsinger, K, & Shafer, M.A. (2009). Predictors of one-year attrition in female Marine Corps recruits. Military Medicine, 174(4): 382-91.

Pressman, S.D., Cohen, S. (2005). Does positive affect influence health? Psychological Bulletin, 131(6): 925-71.

Rounds, M. (2010). The principle challenge of realizing total force fitness: Changing our readiness culture. Military Medicine,175(Suppl 1, August 2010): 124-126.

Southwick, S. (2010). Adapting to stress: Lessons from the resilient. Paper presented at the 2010 Navy and Marine Corps Combat Operational Stress Conference: Taking action, measuring results. May 18-21, 2010, San Diego, CA. Retrieved from http://www.med.navy.mil/sites/nmcsd/

Stander, V.A., Merrill, L.L., Thomsen, C.J., Milner, J.S. (2007). Posttraumatic stress symptoms in Navy personnel: Prevalence rates among recruits in basic training. Journal of Anxiety Disorders, 21(6): 860-70.

Stanley, E., Jha, A. (2009). Mind fitness: Improving operational effectiveness and building warrior resilience. Joint Force Periodical, 55(4): 144-51.

Steginga, S.K., Occhipinti, S. (2006). Dispositional optimism as a predictor of men's decision-related distress after localized prostate cancer. Health Psychology, 25(2): 135-143.

Steptoe, A., O'Donnell, K,, Marmot, M,, Wardle, J. (2008). Positive affect and psychosocial processes related to health. British Journal of Psychology, 99(Pt 2): 211-27.

Total Force Fitness for the 21st Century: A new paradigm. (2010). Military Medicine, 175(Suppl 1, August 2010): 1-126.

Tugade, M.M., Fredrickson, B.L. (2004). Resilient individuals use positive emotions to bounce back from negative emotional experiences. Journal of Personality and Social Psychology, 86(2): 320-33.

Wald, J., Taylor, S., Asmundson, G.J., Jang, K., Stapleton, J. (2006). Literature review of concepts: Psychological resiliency. Retrieved from http://www.dtic.mil/cgi-bin/GetTRDoc?

Westphal, R. (2010). The Okinawa experience: The USNH Okinawa's caregiver occupational stress program. Paper presented at the 2010 Navy and Marine Corps Combat Operational Stress Conference: Taking action, measuring results. May 18-22, 2010, San Diego, CA. 2010.

Williams, A., Hagerty, B.M., Yousha, S.M., Horrocks, J., Hoyle, K.S., & Liu, D. (2004) Psychosocial effects of the BOOT STRAP intervention in Navy recruits. Military Medicine, 169(10): 814-20.

Willis, S. (2010). Joint chiefs chair visits USU: Navy Admiral Mullen addresses total fitness.

Young T. (2005). Population health: Concepts and methods. 2nd ed. New York: Oxford University Press (62)

Legal References

Arizona Revised Statute for Privileged Communications, § 322085 (1965). (Privileged Communications)

Buwa v. Smith, 84 1905 NMB (1986). (Duty to Warn)

Canterbury v. Spense, 464 F. 2d. 772 (D.C. Cir. 1972), cert. den. 93 S.Ct. 560 (1972). (Informed Consent)

Cutter v. Brownbridge, Cal. Ct. App., 1st Dist. 330 (1986). (Privileged Communications)

Hales v. Pittman, 118 Ariz. 305, 576 P. 2d. 493 (1978). (Informed Consent)

McDonald v. Clinger, 446 N.Y.S. 2d. 801 (1982). (Confidentiality)

McIntosh v. Milano, 403 A. 2d. 500 (N.J.S.Ct. 1979). (Duty to Warn)

New Jersey Revised Statutes, New Jersey Marriage Counseling Act, Annotated § 45: 8B 29 (1969). (Exceptions to Confidentiality)*People v. District Court, City and County of Denver*, 719 P. 2d. 722 (Colo. 1986). (Privileged Communications)

Rodriguez v. Jackson, 118 Ariz. 13, 574 P. 2d. 481 (App. 1978). (Informed Consent)

Sard v. Hardy, 291 Md. 432, 379 A. 2d. 1014 (1977). (Informed Consent)

Tarasoff v. Regents of California, 131 Cal. Rptr. 14, 551 P. 2d. 334 (1976). (Duty to Warn)

Whitree v. State of New York, 56 Misc. 2d. 693, 290 N.Y.S. 2s. 486 (1968). (Record Keeping)

Force Protection Bibliography

American Red Cross (2010). *Disaster Frontline Supervisor* Course Fact Sheet (DSSSS601A). Retrieved from https://crossnet.redcross.org/chapters/services/disasters/train/basic/DFS_FactSheet.pdf

American Red Cross (2010) *Coping with Disaster: For Families of Disaster Workers.* H20696B-02/10 (formerly A4474) Retrieved fromhttps://crossnet.redcross.org/chapters/services/disasters/ds_prog_guid/reference_docs/FamiliesOfWorkersBrochure.pdf

American Red Cross (2010) *Coping with Disaster: Preparing for a Disaster Assignment.* H20696C-02/10 Retrieved from https://crossnet.redcross.org/chapters/services/disasters/ds_prog_guid/reference_docs/PreparingDisasterAssign.pdf

American Red Cross (2010). *Coping with Disaster: Returning Home from a Disaster Assignment*. H20696A-02/10 (formerly A4473). Retrieved from https://crossnet.redcross.org/chapters/services/disasters/ds_prog_guid/reference_docs/ReturnHomeDisasterAssignBrochure.pdf

Aten, J.D., Madson, M.B., Rice, A., & Chamberlain, A.K. (2008). Post disaster supervisor strategies for promoting supervisee self-care: Lessons learned from Hurricane Katrina. *Training and Education in Professional Psychology*, 2(2), 75-78.

Dworznik, G. J. (2008) The psychology of local news: Compassion fatigue and post traumatic stress in broadcast reporters, photographers and live truck engineers. *Dissertation Abstracts International*.

Ehring, T., Razik, S. & Emmelkamp, P. (2011) Prevalence and predictors of posttraumatic stress disorder, anxiety, depression and burnout in Pakistani earthquake recovery workers. *Psychiatry Research*, 185, 161-166.

Flannelly, K. J., Roberts, Rabbi S. R., & Weaver, A.J. (2005). Correlates of compassion fatigue and burnout in chaplains and other clergy who responded to the September 11th attacks in New York City. *The Journal of Pastoral Care & Counseling*, 59, 213-224.

Mendenhall, T.J. (2006). Trauma-response teams: Inherent challenges and practical strategies in interdisciplinary fieldwork. *Families, Systems & Health*, 24(3), 357-362.

Mitani, S., Fujita, M., Nakata, K. & Shirakawa, T. (2006) Impact of posttraumatic stress disorder and job-related stress on burnout: A study of fire service workers. *The Journal of Emergency Medicine*, 31, 7-11.

Rosser, B.R.S. (2008). Working as a psychologist in the Medical Reserve Corps: Providing emergency mental health relief services in Hurricanes Katrina and Rita. *Professional Psychology: Research and Practice*, 39(1), 37-44.

Schreiber, M. (2009, January). Managing the psychological impact of mass casualty events: The PsySTART Disaster Systems of Care Incident. Management model. Presentation to Idaho State University, Idaho. Bioterrorism and Preparedness Program.

Steerman, C., Cole, V. (2009). Recruitment and Retention of Red Cross Disaster Volunteers. *The Australasian Journal of Disaster*. No. 2009-1

Yin, R.T. (2004). Innovations in the Management of Child Protection Workers: Building Worker Resilience. Social Health Workers: Force Health Protection Strategies. *Terrorism, Trauma and Tragedies*.

COL JAMES L. GREENSTONE, EdD, JD, DABECI

Dr. Greenstone has been in practice for almost fifty years in Dallas and Fort Worth, Texas, and served as the Police Psychologist and Director of Psychological Services for the Fort Worth Police Department. He has been a police officer for thirty-five years. His work in Crisis Intervention and disaster response began in the mid – 1960's, and continues to this day. He studied with such luminaries in the field as Edward Rosenbluh, Morton Bard, W. Rodney Fowler, Muzafer Sherif, Frank Bolz, Sharon Leviton, Fred Lanceley, Tony Cooper, Kent Rensin, James Oney, Mike McMains and others. He has written widely in this as well as in other areas. He is currently Professor of Disaster and Emergency Preparedness for Nova Southeastern University, College of Osteopathic Medicine. He is a licensed professional counselor, licensed marriage and family therapist, and a dispute mediator and arbitrator. He holds earned degrees in Clinical Psychology, Education, Criminal Justice and Law. He interned at the Devereux Foundation in Devon, Pennsylvania and received advanced training at Harvard Law School.

Dr. Greenstone serves on a Federal Disaster Medical Assistance Team as a Supervisory Mental Health Specialist; served as Colonel and Deputy Commander of the Texas State Guard Medical Brigade, Texas Military Forces. He is a Certified Crisis Intervener, a Certified Traumatologist, an Emergency Medical Technician, and a Master Peace Officer. Dr. Greenstone has earned the Master Military Emergency Management Specialist Qualification.

While with the Fort Worth Police Department Dr. Greenstone supervised the department's Peer Support Team; was the Coordinator of the Critical Incident Stress Management program and as a member of the Department's Hostage and Crisis Negotiation Team served as the Operational Police Behavioral Health Specialist.

Dr. Greenstone is a Diplomate in Crisis Intervention from the American Board of Examiners in Crisis Intervention; a Diplomate in Police Psychology from the Society for Police and Criminal Psychology; a Diplomate of the American Board of Forensic Examiners; a Diplomate in Traumatic Stress from the American Academy of Experts in Traumatic Stress, and a Fellow of the College of The American College of Forensic Examiners. He is a Practitioner Member of the Academy of Family Mediators / Association for Conflict Resolution, is a Diplomate in

Trauma Counseling from the American Mental Health Counselor's Association, and is a Clinical Fellow of the American Association of Marriage and Family Therapists.

Dr. Greenstone is a Colonel in the Texas Military Forces. In 2008, Dr. Greenstone was the recipient of the Military Member of the Year Award from the American Red Cross for his work with deploying and redeploying warriors of our armed forces and their families. He is the recipient of the Army Commendation Medal, the State of Texas Lone Star Distinguished Service Medal, the Texas Outstanding Service Medal, and the Expert Field Medical Badge among others. He was awarded the Outstanding Eagle Scout Award by the National Eagle Scout Association, Boy Scouts of America. Recently, Dr. Greenstone was elected as a Fellow of The Royal Society of Medicine, London, England.

"Where reason is needed, emotions are of little value."

Greenstone, 2011

wholeperson

Whole Person Associates is the leading publisher of training resources for professionals who empower people to create and maintain healthy lifestyles. Our creative resources will help you work effectively with your clients in the areas of stress management, wellness promotion, mental health and life skills.

Please visit us at our web site: **www.wholeperson.com**. You can check out our entire line of products, place an order, request our print catalog, and sign up for our monthly special notifications.

Whole Person Associates

800-247-6789

CPSIA information can be obtained
at www.ICGtesting.com
Printed in the USA
FFOW01n1347310516
24445FF